Autonomous Vehicles and the Law

ELGAR LAW, TECHNOLOGY AND SOCIETY

Series Editor: Peter K. Yu, *Drake University Law School, USA*

The information revolution and the advent of digital technologies have ushered in new social practices, business models, legal solutions, regulatory policies, governance structures, consumer preferences and global concerns. This unique book series provides an interdisciplinary forum for studying the complex inter-actions that arise from this environment. It examines the broader and deeper theoretical questions concerning information law and policy, explores its latest developments and social implications, and provides new ways of thinking about changing technology.

Titles in the series include:

Copyright Law and the Progress of Science and the Useful Arts
Alina Ng

Transnational Culture in the Internet Age
Sean A. Pager and Adam Candeub

Environmental Technologies, Intellectual Property and Climate Change
Accessing, Obtaining and Protecting
Abbe E.L. Brown

Privacy and Legal Issues in Cloud Computing
Edited by Anne S.Y. Cheung and Rolf H. Weber

Intellectual Property and Access to Im/material Goods
Edited by Jessica C. Lai and Antoinette Maget Dominicé

The Legal Challenges of Social Media
Edited by David Mangan and Lorna E. Gillies

Digital Democracy in a Globalized World
Edited by Corlen Prins, Colette Cuijpers, Peter L. Lindseth and Mônica Rosina

Privacy in Public Space
Conceptual and Regulatory Challenges
Edited by Tjerk Timan, Bryce Clayton Newell and Bert-Jaap Koops

Autonomous Vehicles and the Law
Technology, Algorithms and Ethics
Hannah YeeFen Lim

Autonomous Vehicles and the Law
Technology, Algorithms and Ethics

Hannah YeeFen Lim

Associate Professor of Business Law, Nanyang Technological University, Singapore

ELGAR LAW, TECHNOLOGY AND SOCIETY

Edward Elgar
PUBLISHING
Cheltenham, UK • Northampton, MA, USA

Published by
Edward Elgar Publishing Limited
The Lypiatts
15 Lansdown Road
Cheltenham
Glos GL50 2JA
UK

Edward Elgar Publishing, Inc.
William Pratt House
9 Dewey Court
Northampton
Massachusetts 01060
USA

A catalogue record for this book
is available from the British Library

Library of Congress Control Number: 2018954447

This book is available electronically in the **Elgar**online
Law subject collection
DOI 10.4337/9781788115117

ISBN 978 1 78811 510 0 (cased)
ISBN 978 1 78811 511 7 (eBook)

To Him who has given me all good things

Contents

About the author

Hannah YeeFen Lim graduated with double degrees in Computer Science and in Law from the University of Sydney, where she went on to complete a Master of Laws by Research with Honours under a Telstra Scholarship. She is currently an Associate Professor of Business Law at Nanyang Technological University. She was a full-time Visiting Professor at the Faculty of Law, NUS from 2007 to 2011. Prior to that, she taught at the University of Sydney and UNSW. In 2013, she was a Visiting Scholar at the University of Cambridge and in 2010, she was a Visiting Researcher at Berkman Center for Internet & Society, Harvard University.

Hannah is an internationally recognized legal expert in Technology & Internet law, IP law, and Data Protection and Privacy law. She is the author of six scholarly books published by internationally established publishers. She wrote one of the pioneering books on Internet law, *Cyberspace Law* in 2002, published by OUP, and her research has been cited with approval by senior judiciary, most notably by the High Court of Australia. She has also published extensively in internationally well-respected refereed journals.

Preface

As a legal academic driven by the constant search for truth, I grew increasingly uncomfortable with the many exaggerations, half-truths and misconceptions about autonomous vehicles and the technologies behind them that began to appear frequently in the popular press. When these were transferred into academic literature, I became alarmed.

As a computer scientist, I knew that quite a number of the claims and exaggerations were just that. They had little or no foundations. What concerned me was that there appeared to be a tidal wave sweeping up the unsuspecting. Some regulators and well-meaning legal scholars were presenting papers at conferences on autonomous vehicles and artificial intelligence without a proper grasp of the underlying technology. Some made fantastic claims that were not supportable.

This book is an attempt at inter-disciplinary discourse. It is hoped that it will bring about a general understanding of the technologies in an accessible manner and to utilize this understanding to move forward in the task of formulating sound and ethical laws, regulations and policies concerning autonomous vehicles.

I am immensely grateful to Edward Elgar and his entire team of dedicated professionals at his wonderful publishing house, and I thank each of them for their unwavering support, especially Edward Elgar, Laura Mann and Luke Adams.

This book encompasses materials available to me as at 26 May 2018.

Hannah YeeFen Lim
Trinity Sunday, 27 May 2018

1. Introduction

Many claims have been made about autonomous vehicles, from their ability to reduce pollution to their ability to reduce deaths on the roads.[1] Many academic articles have been devoted to this new technology with an almost romantic appeal and science fiction glamor. Many commentators write as if it is a given that autonomous vehicles will never make mistakes and will be safer and will save lives. This is an unsupported and untested assumption routinely made by scholars.[2]

In reality, many of these assumptions are based on hype and an exaggeration of the technology, partly fuelled by those who stand to gain from the hype. There is a considerable gap between the hype and the reality.

Whilst autonomous vehicles may seem to be able to navigate the roads with ease, however surreal that is, the technology is not as advanced as it may appear. The artificial intelligence technology appears intelligent but in reality is without intelligence. As the following chapters will demonstrate, the technology is very much explainable in terms of computer science and mathematics. Contrary to what many people may believe, there is no real intelligence behind the autonomous vehicles or behind artificial intelligence.

Computers are excellent at routine and repetitive tasks. They are also very fast, and so they are able to calculate many iterations in one second. Therefore, it is clear that the tasks where computers will excel are ones that are structured, routine and repetitive. This has already been established in assembly lines, where computers and other machines have replaced humans because they are more efficient than humans at repetition, and they do not become bored or tired like humans do.

---

[1]   See for example, Matthew Blunt, 'Highway to a Headache: Is Tort-Based Automotive Insurance on a Collision Course with Autonomous Vehicles?' (2017) 53 Willamette Law Review 107; Gary E Marchant and Rachel A Lindor, 'The Coming Collision Between Autonomous Vehicles and the Liability System' (2012) 52 Santa Clara Law Review 1321; Erica Palmerini et al, Guidelines on Regulating Robotics (2014) <http://www.robolaw.eu/index.htm> accessed 13 May 2018, 58–60; Tracy Hresko Pearl, 'Fast & Furious: The Misregulation of Driverless Cars' (2017) 73 New York University Annual Survey of American Law 19; Jeffrey Gurney J, 'Crashing into the Unknown: An Examination of Crash-Optimization Algorithms through the Two Lanes of Ethics and Law' (2015–2016) 79 Albany Law Review 183.
[2]   Ibid.

Is driving a vehicle a routine and repetitive task? Yes and no. It is routine and repetitive if it is simply staying on the sealed road within two white lines on a seemingly endless highway. It is not routine when driving through road construction sites with detours and temporary traffic lights, and pedestrians, cyclists and motorcyclists all likely to be present or suddenly appearing in your lane.

It is true that computer science and in particular, artificial intelligence have advanced greatly. Similarly, there have been huge advancements in computational power and storage. More recently, the explosion of available big data has also enabled data analytics research to soar. These are the reasons why autonomous vehicles have burst on the scene recently. With the advancements in computational power and storage, far more complex mathematical and statistical models have been constructed to process big data, to enable probability and other calculations to be made that will assist an autonomous vehicle to determine whether the object in front of it is likely to be a flying paper bag that it can safely ignore or a large truck that it should immediately swerve to avoid. This is how an autonomous vehicle is able to achieve some semblance of driving in unpredictable conditions.

As the following chapters will reveal, autonomous vehicles rely on material and physical sciences, mathematics and statistics thrown together but set within the framework of computer programs. There is no magic to it. The limitations are also quite obvious.

At the present time, the key draw of autonomous vehicles is not that they are safer than human drivers, as many would like to believe, but the convenience of not having to drive. Many of the so-called safety features on autonomous vehicles can be or are already on conventional vehicles. Such safety features include collision warning systems, adaptive cruise control systems and emergency braking systems. These are the systems that prevent accidents and save lives. If there is technology that can detect the alcohol level of drivers, perhaps through their breath, and immobilize the vehicle if they are drunk, that would also be a helpful safety feature for conventional vehicles. Similarly, eye tracking software can also be installed on conventional vehicles to ensure that drivers are not texting or otherwise not paying attention to the road. These systems on all conventional vehicles would go a long way towards reducing accidents and traffic deaths.

At present, autonomous vehicles present many new safety threats and their proper regulation should be a top priority for consumer safety advocates, lawyers, regulators, ethicists and industry officials. There have been a number of accidents and deaths involving autonomous systems, demonstrating that questions must be raised as to whether it is right to release the currently imperfect versions of autonomous vehicle technology onto public roads, even when there are people behind the wheel who are meant to take control in dangerous situations.

Much of the existing literature on regulation of autonomous vehicles has been written by legal scholars who do not understand the technology and they assume that autonomous vehicles are just as the manufacturers have claimed them to be.

This book will attempt to set the facts straight. It will explain how autonomous vehicles function, including highlighting their inherent limitations. A clear understanding of the technology is essential as it is only when one understands something and knows how it works that one can properly and appropriately regulate it. Otherwise, the discussion will be superficial, tiptoeing around the subject matter with assumptions that turn out to be quite wrong. The accessible exposition of the technologies provides a sound basis upon which legal arguments and regulatory decisions can be made.

Once the technical foundations have been laid, the remaining chapters will assess the relevant current legal standards that are applicable to the technical parts of an autonomous vehicle and suggest appropriate regulatory and ethical approaches that can be taken, as well as canvassing the ethical considerations and responsibilities.

It is not the aim of this modest work to cover all areas related to autonomous vehicles; hence discourse on data protection, insurance, intellectual property laws and many other areas will not be included.

2.   How autonomous vehicles function

This chapter will provide an overview of how autonomous vehicles function. The purpose here is not to carve out a technical manual of the functionality of autonomous vehicles. Instead, knowledge about how autonomous vehicles function will be crucial in identifying the legal and ethical issues posed by them and discerning how they ought to be regulated.

At the outset, the distinction between a semi-autonomous and a fully autonomous vehicle must be made. They sit on a continuum of automation levels, which the US Department of Transportation and the National Highway Traffic Safety Administration have adopted[1] from the Society of Automotive Engineers International classification. The six levels range from Level 0 to Level 5 and they are as follows:[2]

- *Level 0 (no automation):* There is no automation and the driver is in complete and sole control of the vehicle and performs all tasks associated with driving.
- *Level 1 (driver assistance):* The vehicle is controlled by the driver and the majority of the work is done by the person at the wheel, but some driving assist features may be included in the vehicle design. Hence, the driver and a computer system work together on tasks. An example of this found in many cars today is cruise control.
- *Level 2 (partial automation):* The vehicle has combined automated functions, for example, the steering and speed of the vehicle are controlled by one or more driver-assistance systems but a human controls the other elements of driving. Hence, the human driver must remain engaged with the driving task and monitor the environment at all times. Examples of this found in cars today are the self-parking feature, lane-keeping systems and emergency braking systems.
- *Level 3 (conditional automation):* Vehicles in Level 3 and above are considered 'automated driving systems'. The vehicles at this level and higher

---

[1]   US Department of Transportation and the National Highway Traffic Safety Administration, *Automated Driving Systems (ADS): A Vision for Safety 2.0* (2017) <https://www.nhtsa.gov/sites/nhtsa.dot.gov/files/documents/13069a-ads2.0_090617_v9a_tag.pdf> accessed 21 April 2018.

[2]   Ibid. 4.

are able to monitor the driving environment around them – a driver is necessary, but is not required to monitor the environment. The driver must however be ready to take control of the vehicle at all times with notice. Typically, these types of vehicles can and do make decisions themselves. For instance, a Level 3 car will be capable of seeing a slower moving vehicle in front of it before making a decision to decelerate or overtake.

- *Level 4 (high automation):* The vehicle is capable of performing all driving functions under certain conditions, that is, specific driving modes. The vehicle will stop itself if the systems fail. The driver may have the option to control the vehicle, especially when conditions confuse predefined use cases, such as road works or road diversions, or when the driver desires to.
- *Level 5 (full automation):* The vehicle is capable of performing all driving functions under all conditions; no human control of a vehicle is needed. The driver may have the option to control the vehicle but is not expected to be available for control at any time during the trip. Level 5 vehicles have full automation and vehicles do not require any pedals, steering wheels or controls for a human to take charge. The computer controlled systems of the vehicle make important choices about their own actions with little or no human intervention – independent decision making is the key. Often, the human's role is limited to inputting the destination. Level 5 vehicles are able to manage or direct their own activities, even in the event of an unpredictable or changing physical environment. The race in this space is purportedly, in early 2018, led by Google, through its Waymo subsidiary, and General Motors with its subsidiary Cruise Automation.[3]

This book will be predominantly concerned with vehicles in Level 5, that is, fully autonomous vehicles, although the technologies and considerations will also be relevant to vehicles in Levels 2–4.

2.1. THE PROCESS: SENSE–PLAN–ACT

In order for a fully autonomous vehicle to drive itself from one location to another completely on its own, without any human intervention, the autonomous vehicle must necessarily make many major driving decisions and successfully carry out operations including steering, acceleration, braking, appropriate driving speed, judging the distance between vehicles, choosing the correct lane and the route and, of course, avoiding obstacles.

---

[3] Phil LeBeau, 'Inside the race to deliver the first self-driving car', *CNBC* (10 March 2018) <https://www.cnbc.com/2018/03/10/waymo-gm-still-lead-the-self-driving-car-race.html> accessed 21 April 2018.

For an autonomous vehicle to be able to make all these decisions and to successfully carry them out, most autonomous vehicle systems adopt a sense, plan and act process.[4] Within each of these stages, there are many sub-stages. For example, sensing the surrounding will first require the autonomous vehicle to sense physically that some things or objects are around it, then it will need to perceive or understand what those objects are.

On board autonomous vehicles are many devices, such as sensors, which continuously collect raw data about the outside world, that is, the road and surrounding environment. The raw data is then analysed by the autonomous vehicle's software algorithms, such as identifying the lane markings from the images of the road. At this analysis stage, much data from different sensors may need to be integrated to accurately interpret the physical surroundings,[5] for example, the imaging sensor's data will need to be integrated with another sensor which can detect the physical presence of physical objects to confirm that the white markings are indeed lane markings and not some barrier or kerb or gutter.

These data are used in the planning stage to plan the vehicle's own actions about where it should safely move next, including immediate decisions such as steering directions and speed, as well as more distant decisions such as the overall route. These plans are then executed as commands to the vehicle's control systems and implemented as actions such as apply the brakes, steer to the right, and so on.

This sense–plan–act process loop is continuously occurring, being repeated thousands of times per second. The process loop will run in parallel for many of the on-board devices. Some loops will run at higher frequencies than others. The devices that detect obstacles, for example, will need to run at extremely high frequencies to enable rapid detection of obstacles and apply emergency braking or cancel a lane change. In this scenario, the cycle may be shortened to just a sense–and–act cycle as the planning stage of the loop is extremely short.[6]

How these devices are designed, how the algorithmic analysis is performed and how they interact with each other will be crucial in determining the decision made by the autonomous vehicle, which will in turn be fundamentally important in questions of liability.

---

[4]   James M Anderson et al, *Autonomous Vehicle Technology: A Guide for Policymakers* (Rand Corp 2016), 58.
[5]   Harry Surden and Mary-Anne Williams, 'Techonological opacity, predictability, and self-driving cars' (2016) 38 Cardozo Law Review 121, 141.
[6]   James M Anderson et al (n 4), 59.

2.2.   THE CHALLENGES OF SENSING

For an autonomous vehicle to perform safely in a human-centric environment, it must be able to sense and make sense of the complex and dynamic driving environment. Not only does an autonomous vehicle need to be aware of the static terrain, it also needs to be aware of many moving and non-static objects, obstacles and people, and to be able to predict their location in the immediate future. The complex array of the dynamic driving environment comprises other moving vehicles on the road, pedestrians, cyclists and motorcyclists, all of which move at different speeds, as well as animals and even debris, such as that from traffic accidents. Weather conditions can also hamper an autonomous vehicle's perception of its surroundings, for example, rain and snow will affect its ability to distinguish objects. If there are road works, or slight detours resulting from construction or an accident, or poorly marked roads, all of these will negatively affect the autonomous vehicle's ability to function.

Humans are equipped with an intellect and eyes, which are both critical for the task of driving. Humans can understand and interpret driving features such as traffic lights, stop signs and lane markings. An autonomous vehicle needs to be able to distinguish these and to recognize shapes and classify moving objects such as cars, bicycles, animals and pedestrians. Most autonomous vehicles use a range of computer vision systems and sensors to assist in the sensing of objects. These will now be considered.

2.2.1.   Camera-based Systems

Camera-based systems are the first line in an autonomous vehicle's system of sensing. Cameras are inexpensive and the images collected by the vehicle's cameras can be used by the software algorithms to compare and conduct analysis with a pre-built databank of images of the surroundings.

Long-range cameras can provide extensive long-distance views of the surroundings. However, the algorithms that interpret camera images may not be accurate in distinguishing or categorizing objects when the ambient conditions are not ideal, such as at nighttime, in bright sunlight, where there are abrupt lighting changes (e.g. entering and exiting tunnels) and in heavy rain or snow. The artificial intelligence system may have difficulty interpreting images when the databank it has been trained on utilizes images taken on predominantly clear sunny days and not in torrential downpours where visibility is poor.

Video cameras can be used to determine the location and speed of objects. If multiple video cameras are placed around an autonomous vehicle, enabling them to receive parallel images of the same object from different angles, this enables the vehicle's computer to estimate an object's distance. Typically, an autonomous vehicle would have a rear and several 360 degree cameras. In many of the newer cars on the market, two-dimensional cameras have been supplied by the manufacturer to display images and sometimes superimpose additional information on the display, such as the steering wheel angle and the path of the vehicle if the steering wheel angle is maintained. More commonly known as surround-view cameras, the system functions by having cameras on all four sides and the on-board computer stitches together a birds-eye view of the vehicle from overhead and shows a moving image on a screen, along with the surroundings such as parking space lane markings and adjacent cars.[7]

On autonomous vehicles, in order for the three-dimensional image to be realistic, usually the input signals from four to six cameras are required. Image sensors must have very high dynamic range in order to deliver a clear image even with direct sunlight shining into the lens.[8]

Forward-facing camera systems are typically for medium to high ranges of up to 250 metres. These cameras use software algorithms to detect objects, classify them and determine the distance from them. The cameras can identify pedestrians, cyclists and vehicles but they can and have been in error where pictures of people and cyclists are on the paintwork of other vehicles, thus demonstrating one of the key weaknesses of cameras.[9] Software algorithms are also used to help detect traffic signals and the colour of the signals (red or green), as well as traffic signs, and read the words on the signs.

Typically, medium-range cameras are used to detect more immediate situations such as crossing traffic, pedestrians and even emergency braking in the car ahead, whereas long-range cameras are used for traffic sign recognition, video-based distance control and road guidance.

---

[7]   Bill Howard, 'What are car surround view cameras, and why are they better than they need to be?', *Extremetech* (18 July 2014) <https://www.extremetech.com/ extreme/186160-what-are-surround-view-cameras-and-why-are-they-better-than-they -need-to-be/2> accessed 23 April 2018.

[8]   Gert Rudolph and Uwe Voelzke, 'Three sensor types drive autonomous vehicles' (10 November 2017) <https://www.sensorsmag.com/components/three-sensor-types -drive-autonomous-vehicles> accessed 23 April 2018.

[9]   Jamie Condliffe, 'This image is why self-driving cars come loaded with many types of sensors', *MIT Technology Review* (21 July 2017) <https://www .technologyreview.com/s/608321/this-image-is-why-self-driving-cars-come-loaded -with-many-types-of-sensors/> accessed 23 April 2018.

2.2.2.   Lidar Systems

Lidar (light detection and ranging) systems have been touted as the most important piece of hardware for self-driving cars[10] and were the subject of the now settled legal action that Google's subsidiary Waymo commenced in February 2017 against Uber for patent infringement and trade secret theft in the US.[11] Lidar is used to determine distances to objects by emitting millions of laser beams every second and measuring how long it takes the laser beams to reflect off the objects. Lidar is extremely accurate. Many sophisticated lidars comprise multiple laser range finders with rapidly rotating mirrors to generate three-dimensional data point clouds of the surrounding environment. These point clouds are used to create a three-dimensional 'map' of the area surrounding the vehicle. The point clouds and three-dimensional 'map' are compared with a reference three-dimensional map of the area created from humans pre-driving the area using lidars, to determine what may have changed. These reference maps often have detailed images of each section of the road location, including lane markings. Using these point clouds and map, the software algorithms can (or should be able to) ascertain cyclists, pedestrians and other vehicles, whilst ignoring unimportant objects that may have changed, such as flying birds.

Advanced lidars can also track the objects as they move.[12] Indeed, this would be a crucial functionality for a moving vehicle. If an autonomous vehicle detects a pedestrian pushing a bicycle in the near distance and moving perpendicular to the path of the vehicle, it needs to be able to predict where the pedestrian and bicycle will be a few moments later by analyzing the pedestrian's and bicycle's current speed and direction relative to its future position. If the pedestrian and bicycle and the vehicle are likely to intersect, then the autonomous vehicle must take action, such as applying the brakes or swerving. This was exactly the scenario in the fatal Uber crash in Tempe, Arizona in March 2018. The Uber autonomous vehicle crashed into and killed a pedestrian pushing a bicycle across the road at night without slowing down at all.

---

[10]   Alex Davies, 'What is Lidar, why do self-driving cars need it, and can it see nerf bullets?', *Wired* (6 February 2018) <https://www.wired.com/story/lidar-self-driving-cars-luminar-video/> accessed 21 April 2018.

[11]   Biz Carson, 'Everyone walked away a winner in Uber–Waymo settlement, but most of the damage had already been done', *Forbes* (13 February 2018) <https://www.forbes.com/sites/bizcarson/2018/02/13/everyone-walked-away-a-winner-in-uber-waymo-settlement-but-most-of-the-damage-had-already-been-done/#53f85b22fcf7> accessed 23 April 2018.

[12]   Alex Davies (n 10).

This incident, including the questions of liability and ethics, will be discussed further in Chapters 3 and 6 respectively.

Lidars are typically mounted on top of vehicles, amongst other positions, to achieve, as far as possible, an unobstructed view as the lidar continuously and rapidly spins through 360 degrees to capture possible objects on all sides. As lidars continue to collect data and generate the point clouds, a phenomenal amount of data is accumulated which can then be used to further improve the algorithmic performance of the artificial intelligence software.

The point clouds and three-dimensional maps enable the autonomous vehicle to locate its position with greater accuracy than commercial global positioning systems (GPS), which have limitations, as will be discussed below.[13] GPS can, however, be used by the autonomous vehicle to determine its approximate location, which enables it to retrieve pre-created maps of the nearby area. The maps can be compared with the live lidar scans of the surrounding area to determine, probabilistically, where the autonomous vehicle is likely to be on the map.[14] This process of geographic location determination is known as 'localization'. In summary, lidar is used to both detect objects surrounding the vehicles, as well as determining the exact location of the autonomous vehicle.

Lidars have a notable advantage over cameras in that they can also function at night. The resolution of lidar is better than that of radar and it is able to identify objects such as arms and hands with precision.[15] One of the first lidars to be used in autonomous vehicles is the Velodyne HDL-64E lidar, which uses 64 lasers providing 1.3 million data points per second with a 360 degree field of view.[16] Lidars are, however, practically useful only over short ranges with the Velodyne providing data up to 120 metres away, depending on the reflectivity of the object.[17] Objects with poor reflectivity such as black asphalt can only be detected by the Velodyne to a range of 50 metres.[18] White lane markings painted on the roads that are reflective can be detected with great precision in dry conditions, which is extremely useful in keeping the autonomous vehicle within its lane as it drives itself.

An autonomous vehicle typically will have numerous lidars on-board; the more lidars it has, the more accurate it will be in detecting obstacles and in

---

[13]   See Section 2.2.5.
[14]   Christoph Mertz, Luis E Navarro-Serment, Robert MacLachlan, Paul Rybski, Aaron Steinfeld, Arne Suppé, Christopher Urmson, Nicolas Vandapel, Martial Hebert, Chuck Thorpe, David Duggins and Jay Gowdy, 'Moving object detection with laser scanners' (2013) 30 Journal of Field Robotics 17.
[15]   Alex Davies (n 10).
[16]   James M Anderson et al (n 4), 61–62.
[17]   Ibid.
[18]   Ibid.

determining its location. As will be argued in Chapter 3, the number of lidars will be crucial in the design of autonomous vehicles in meeting safety and ethical standards.

2.2.3. Radar Systems

Radar systems have different capabilities and limitations from lidars; radars are not as accurate as lidars but they have other advantages. Radar systems emit radio waves to determine the presence of objects. Radars measure the time it takes for the radio waves to reflect off surfaces in order to determine the position of the object. The location, speed, movement and direction of an object can be calculated through the angle, timing and strength of the reflected wave. Radar works well on metallic objects, such as vehicles, but non-metallic objects, such as pedestrians, cannot be detected by a radar sensor.[19]

Radars have a much greater range than lidars and can detect objects 200 metres away, and as such, they are useful for assessing the speed of multiple moving objects that are around the autonomous vehicle, such as other vehicles.[20] Radars are inexpensive when compared with lidars and many modern cars today have radars fitted on them, especially on the front and rear bumpers to avoid collisions.

Whilst the detection range of radars is higher than that of lidars, radars are not very accurate, with measurements often out by several inches to feet in detecting the location of objects.[21] They do, however, provide a good feedback loop of data for lidars owing to their longer range. Autonomous vehicles that are designed for safety will use both radars and lidars, so that they have a better idea of their surrounding environment.

2.2.4. Infrared Systems

Infrared systems may be a vital component in detecting humans and animals on the roads. Passive infrared vision detects differences in the heat emitted by objects. Warm-blooded humans and animals will naturally be easily detected whilst road surfaces can be distinguished from vegetation. Infrared systems provide visual information, as well as the two-dimensional shape of objects.

Since infrared systems do not require light to operate, nor are they affected by oncoming headlights, they are ideal for providing night vision to auton-

---

[19] James M Anderson et al (n 4), 62.
[20] Ryan Whitwam, 'How Google's self-driving cars detect and avoid obstacles', *Extremetech* (8 September 2014) <http://www.extremetech.com/extreme/189486 -howgoogles-self-driving-cars-detect-and-avoid-obstacles> accessed 23 April 2018.
[21] Harry Surden and Mary-Anne Williams (n 5), 145.

omous vehicles. Infrared systems are also unaffected by direct sunlight and abrupt lighting changes, such as when entering or exiting a tunnel, nor do they require clear visibility to function. Thus, they would complement cameras, which are inadequate in these scenarios.[22]

An Israeli company, AdaSky, claims that it has developed an infrared system with a higher resolution of 0.3 megapixels which can operate continuously at 60 frames per second and which can identify pedestrians, cyclists and animals a long way beyond the range of a car's headlights.[23]

2.2.5.   Other Devices

There are a number of other devices and sensors that manufacturers may use to equip autonomous vehicles with a better sense of their surrounding environment. These include GPS, ultrasonic sensors, inertial measurement units and wheel encoders, used to determine the vehicle's location and keep track of its movements.[24]

GPS systems receive signals from satellites to triangulate their global coordinates. These coordinates are usually only accurate down to 4 or 5 metres and are not precise enough for autonomous driving purposes, which require a precision of only a few centimeters. An error of position by 10 or 20 centimeters could place the autonomous vehicle into the neighbouring or oncoming lane. Using GPS alone to determine location would result in it being inaccurate by several metres, even under ideal conditions.[25]

The inaccuracies of GPS grow rapidly when obstacles such as tall buildings or even the natural terrain prevent GPS receivers from obtaining signals from a sufficient number of satellites. Instead, GPS is used as a tool to assist the autonomous vehicle to gain a more precise location by first giving an estimate of the location and then using lidars and three-dimensional maps to obtain pinpoint accuracy of the location. In essence, the GPS coordinates are cross-referenced with three-dimensional maps of the roads or surrounding environment to enable vehicles to identify their positions.

---

[22]   Mark Harris, 'Night vision for self-driving cars', *IEEE Spectrum* (18 October 2017)   <https://spectrum.ieee.org/cars-that-think/transportation/self-driving/do-self driving-cars-need-night-vision> accessed 23 April 2018.
[23]   Ibid.
[24]   Erico Guizzo, 'How Google's self-driving car works', *IEEE Spectrum* (18 October 2011) <https://spectrum.ieee.org/automaton/robotics/artificial-intelligence/how-google-self-driving-car-works> accessed 23 April 2018.
[25]   Ibid. See also Samuel K Moore, 'Superaccurate GPS chips coming to smartphones in 2018', *IEEE Spectrum* (21 September 2017) <https://spectrum.ieee.org/tech-talk/semiconductors/design/superaccurate-gps-chips-coming-to-smartphones-in-2018> accessed 23 April 2018.

Ultrasonic sensors can provide accurate short-range data from 1 to 10 metres, which makes them useful for parking assistance systems and backup warning systems. However, research has shown that ultrasonic sensors have potential vulnerabilities when they are blocked or interfered with by another ultrasonic sensor in the vicinity.[26]

An inertial measurement unit, or IMU, is an electronic device that measures a vehicle's velocity, orientation and gravitational forces, using a combination of accelerometers, gyroscopes and possibly also magnetometers.[27] IMUs have been used to manoeuvre flying objects such as aircraft and unmanned aerial vehicles.[28]

2.2.6.   High-definition Digital Maps

As mentioned above, lidar systems rely on three-dimensional maps as reference maps. These maps have become a key component of autonomous vehicle systems, so much so that China's largest Internet search company, Baidu, has stated that it could be largely a map maker in the future as it begins to sell high-definition (HD) maps for autonomous vehicles as a service.[29]

The HD maps that are built for autonomous vehicles usually have extremely high precision at centimetre-level accuracy for precision.[30] They typically have detailed, road-level images of most street locations, such as the overhead and street-level layouts of roads, including traffic signs and signals, footpaths and of course the associated GPS coordinates.

The maps are usually constructed using 360 degree laser scans of roads from lidars and other sensors, taken from the ground-level perspective of a vehicle. For an HD map to be comprehensive, there must be more than a one-time pre-driving of the roads to collect and aggregate the data to construct the map.

---

[26]   Bing Shun Lim, Sye Loong Keoh and Vrizlynn L L Thing, 'Autonomous vehicle ultrasonic sensor vulnerability and impact assessment', IEEE World Forum on Internet of Things (WF-IoT) 2018, A*STAR Open Access Repository <http://oar.a-star.edu.sg:80/jspui/handle/123456789/2321> accessed 23 April 2018.

[27]   Harsha Vardhan, 'Inertial measurement unit', *Geospatial World* (8 July 2016) <https://www.geospatialworld.net/entity/inertial-measurement-unit/> accessed 23 April 2018.

[28]   Ibid.

[29]   Rachel Metz, 'Baidu sees maps for self-driving cars as bigger business than web search', *MIT Technology Review* (9 January 2018) <https://www.technologyreview.com/s/609936/baidu-sees-maps-for-self-driving-cars-as-bigger-business-than-web-search/> accessed 23 April 2018.

[30]   Harsha Vardhan, 'HD Maps: New age maps powering autonomous vehicles', *Geospatial World* (22 September 2017) <https://www.geospatialworld.net/blogs/hd-maps-autonomous-vehicles/> accessed 23 April 2018.

As each autonomous vehicle drives that section of the road, the maps created by it can be added to the reference HD maps and aggregated for use by autonomous vehicles in the future. In a similar manner, HD maps can be updated dynamically using the live scans of autonomous vehicles. For example, the software engineer can program the system in such a way that if a set number of vehicles have confirmed data that a new set of traffic lights has been installed at an intersection, then the HD map should be dynamically updated. However, software engineers will need to set an appropriate number to trigger the update as programming decisions such as these will be subject to ethics and legal review.

A crucial point to note is that the maps must be maintained. If there are changes on the road, such as road works on a single-lane road, then the autonomous vehicle may not be able to handle the situation, other than perhaps stopping the vehicle if there is a physical barrier in front of it. Needless to say, if there are no HD maps, the autonomous vehicle will have a difficult time navigating the road, which is perhaps why Baidu has made the bold statement that its business in map making will overtake its current business as a search engine.[31]

The HD maps are used by an autonomous vehicle as it travels on the roads, retrieving the HD maps and comparing them with the 'live' map it constructs with its on-board sensors and devices as it arrives at each location. Human map specialists manually annotate the HD maps with important driving information such as traffic lights, signs and lane markings. These assist the autonomous vehicle in detecting and responding to them as it reaches each location. For example, if the HD map indicates a traffic light ahead, the autonomous vehicle can be programmed to slow down, double check that there is indeed a traffic light ahead and check the colour of the traffic light (red or green) to determine whether it should proceed or stop completely. Thus, the HD maps assist the autonomous vehicle to plan and drive better and more safely. If the autonomous vehicle did not use HD maps at all, it would have to rely on the lidars, radars and on-board visual cameras, which may result in it having difficulty in identifying objects and making errors,[32] for example, in approaching a traffic light, as they can sometimes be visually obscured from certain angles by trees, flying birds and other objects. If the visual field is obscured, it will be more challenging for the vehicle to identify if the object in front of it is indeed

---

[31]   Rachel Metz (n 29).

[32]   Vince Bond, Jr, 'Up-to-the-minute maps will be critical for autonomous cars', *Automotive News* (13 September 2014) <http://www.autonews.com/article/20140913/OEM06/309159962/up-to-the-minute-maps-will-be-critical-for-autonomous-vehicles> accessed 23 April 2018.

a traffic light, as it could be some other object on a metal pole. For this reason, HD maps are an essential safety tool.

2.2.7. Algorithms Used in Sensing

The devices discussed above collect massive amounts of data about the environment. Software is still needed to process the data collected and to make sense out of the masses of data. This process could be described as perceiving or understanding what has been physically sensed. For example, how does the autonomous vehicle conclude that the object ahead is a traffic light? There are of course many layers involved in the autonomous vehicle coming to this conclusion. At the most basic level, each device must be sure of what it is reporting to the central control system of the autonomous vehicle; for example, the infrared sensor needs to reliably report that the object ahead is made of metal and is therefore not a human and the radar sensor will also report that the object is made from metal and so on. From there, a second layer requires the autonomous vehicle's central control system to act on the combined data received, possibly passing some data back to one or more of the devices to double confirm it, or feeding the data to an artificial intelligence (AI) system to classify the image. Therefore, continuing on from the traffic light example, the central control system may pass data received from the cameras to an AI pattern recognition algorithm to classify and identify the object.

The above description is a much simplified iteration of what might be happening a million times a second inside the autonomous vehicle in many of its devices. The purpose here is to highlight that continuous processing of data is occurring, and that the processing is often done by an AI system during the sensing phase of operations.

AI systems are being rapidly developed by many organizations but their reliability is still questionable, as they have been known to succeed amazingly or fail spectacularly. Examples of where AI has failed miserably can be found in a research paper published in 2015 on fooling neural networks.[33] In this research, the researchers tested the reliability of state-of-the-art deep neural networks in recognizing objects. The researchers evolved regular images to form abstract ones and tested them on deep neural networks. The results were quite laughable; amongst some of the research results, the deep neural networks classified yellow and black horizontal stripes as a school bus without

---

[33] Anh Nguyen, Jason Yosinski and Jeff Clune, 'Deep neural networks are easily fooled: High confidence predictions for unrecognizable images' in Computer Vision and Pattern Recognition (CVPR '15) (IEEE 2015).

any need for it to have a windscreen or wheels or any of the other characteristics of a real bus.

2.3.   THE PLANNING PHASE

The foregoing has attempted to demonstrate the challenges an autonomous vehicle faces in sensing the surrounding environment. This section will elucidate how the vehicle plans and decides its movements.

Armed with data from the sensing phase, the autonomous vehicle must understand all of the information about its surrounding environment to plan a move. This is possibly where most of the trade secrets lie. Most companies will not reveal how the algorithms or AI systems on their autonomous vehicles function. This is understandable as each company attempts to win the race of developing the first reliable fully autonomous vehicle. From a societal, legal and consumer perspective, however, it is necessary to be given a reasonable explanation of how the AI system functions, as well as tests and assurances that the AI system will function as described and not malfunction. After all, if autonomous vehicles will be deployed on public roads in a mass market manner, the safety of the whole society is at stake, not just those inside the autonomous vehicle.

In the sensing stage, the autonomous vehicle will have rendered the surrounding environment. This would include object detection and object identification or, at the very least, object classification. In the planning stage, the autonomous vehicle requires information that will pinpoint exactly where the object is, commonly known as object localization as well as information on the prediction of movement, if any. This, of course, needs to be done for all objects by each of the available on-board devices, sensors and other equipment, so that for objects such as traffic lights there will be no movement, but for motorcyclists, bicycles and pedestrians their exact locations must be pinpointed and, based on their direction, speed and other factors, their trajectories mapped. The trajectories may be mapped by more than one device or sensor. This will require the AI system of device or sensor to process a great deal of mathematics and return a probabilistic answer on where the object will probably be a few moments later. All of this data is then perhaps fed to another AI system, which will decide where to move or to simply apply the brakes – the autonomous vehicle must after all be notified of all the predictions of possible changes to its surroundings by all of its devices, sensors and algorithms.

How an AI system decides where to move the autonomous vehicle next depends largely on the developers of the autonomous vehicle. The developers regard this as their prized intellectual property and trade secret. AI systems can be solely used to make this decision, or it may be made by a combination of hard-coded programming and an AI algorithm. An example of the latter may look like this: if the lidars and the radars both report that there is or will be an object in the direct path of the vehicle, and the object is on the road surface itself within the lane on which the autonomous vehicle is travelling, then apply the brakes and do not let the AI system make any decisions.

If AI algorithms are used, some of the possible methods are set out below. These are by no means the only methodologies that could be used but they are the more obvious ones that have been revealed by researchers or which are intuitive to any computer scientist.

Decision matrix algorithms are one of the most obvious algorithms that could be employed at this planning stage. This type of algorithm is good at systematically identifying, analyzing and rating the performance of relationships between sets of values and information.[34] Hence, they are effective in processing all of the values and data given to them by the various sensors, devices and other AI algorithms on-board the autonomous vehicle. For example, the classification, recognition and prediction of the next movement of objects all have a confidence level attached, which is essentially the level of confidence each of the algorithms, sensors and devices has in the accuracy of the classification, recognition and prediction of the next movement of objects. Decision matrix algorithms process all of this information from all of the devices, sensors and other algorithms through mathematical and statistical calculations, often through models composed of multiple decision models which have been independently trained.[35] The multiple decision models are used to minimize the possibility of errors in decision making.[36] The most commonly used algorithms are gradient boosting and AdaBoosting.[37]

The training of the multiple decision models can be done through machine learning. Machine learning can be done through a number of methods. Machines and computer programs function by following rules or instructions. In machine learning, in a very general sense, the computer can create its own rules for it to follow. It must, however, be stressed at this point that in creating its own rules, the computer is also largely dictated by how the algorithm has been constructed, including the mathematical and statistical rules that have been used. More details on machine learning will be discussed in Chapter 4.

Machine learning functions by analyzing data and detecting patterns in that data, patterns which may assist the particular task. For example, an algorithm may be training on the basic task of driving, in the artificial scenario of having

---

[34] Anshul Saxena, 'Machine learning algorithms in self-driving cars', *Visteon Technology News* (2 March 2017) <http://visteon.bg/2017/03/02/machine-learning-algorithms-autonomous-cars/> accessed 29 April 2018.
[35] Ibid.
[36] Ibid.
[37] Ibid.

no other objects or people near it. This may involve the algorithm finding the pattern for itself that the vehicle is always driving or situated between two parallel white lines, which we humans would call lane markings. After creating this rule of staying within the two parallel white lines for itself, the algorithm will then always plan to steer the car in whatever direction will maintain the vehicle between the two parallel white lines. If the road is straight, the two parallel white lines will be straight, hence little movement in the directions of steering is required. If the road is slightly curved, the algorithm will make the decision to turn the steering wheel in such directions and angles that will keep the vehicle within the two parallel white lines.

To be complete, it should be clarified that this rule of staying within the two parallel white lines does not need to come from an AI algorithm, nor does it need to utilize machine learning and be 'trained' into the AI algorithm. It can easily also be pre-programmed into the autonomous vehicle's decision-making system. Hence, for this reason, for the question of liability, it is imperative that the facts are clear about how a particular autonomous vehicle functions, so as to properly apportion or find liability.

Returning to the decision matrix algorithms in autonomous vehicles, such algorithms will have to deal with the situation where conflicting data is reported to it by two or more of its on-board devices or sensors. For example, the autonomous vehicle's cameras may report that there is no object ahead, its radars may report there is no obstacle ahead but its lidars report that there is an obstacle ahead with a 70% confidence level. Given that radars cannot detect non-metallic objects such as humans, the decision matrix algorithm will need to process the negative report from the radars alongside with the negative report from its cameras juxtaposed with the positive report from its lidars and calculate statistically or probabilistically whether there is an obstacle ahead and, based on this calculation, decide on the course of action, such as braking, swerving or slowing down to collect more data as the point of interest comes closer.

From this example, it should be abundantly clear that the foundation of the decision-making process is largely mathematics, namely statistics. This is a point that should always be borne in mind in any examination of the legal and ethical issues in any AI application.

2.4.   THE ACTION PHASE

The acting phase is when the autonomous vehicle executes the driving actions that have been issued. The autonomous vehicle may have been instructed by the vehicle's main computer system to accelerate, brake, steer and so on. It should be stressed that, even though a set of instructions may have been issued for the autonomous vehicle to act on, the whole sense–plan–act process is still continuing concurrently. So, even if the instruction is for the autonomous vehicle to accelerate, and the vehicle accelerates, this can be overridden seconds later should an obstacle be detected, so that the instructions a few seconds later may be to activate the brake mechanism.

3. Verifiable standards of care

This chapter will focus on the verifiable standards of care pertaining to autonomous vehicles. Chapter 4 will focus on the standards of care that are less easy to verify.

This taxonomy is devised by this author who also believes it is absolutely essential as the components that make up an autonomous vehicle, or any other AI machines for that matter, will have parts that are scientifically verifiable in terms of material science or other physical sciences. For this reason, since the properties of the materials and devices used by the AI machine are ascertainable and verifiable, the standards of care for those components, and combinations of those components, can be easily and objectively set so as to not cause harm, or at least, set to minimize harm.

This chapter will map out some of the more common fault lines of autonomous vehicles and set them within a loose framework of negligence jurisprudence. The aim here is not to expound the law of negligence as it is conceived in various jurisdictions, rather, it is to use the concepts and the standards found in the tort of negligence to help inform and guide the principles for regulating autonomous vehicles, and to perhaps set a benchmark of acceptable best practices, but without stifling innovation.

Other areas of laws such as product liability laws could also inform the discourse but since the product liability laws in many jurisdictions can differ quite significantly, a common denominator is lacking. In a similar vein, principles from consumer protection laws may also be helpful but some jurisdictions such as Australia[1] provide fairly strong consumer protection laws, whilst other jurisdictions may have none. Hence, since many jurisdictions have a vague understanding of the tort of negligence, negligence shall be used to provide the loose framework for the discourse.

This chapter will first elucidate the relevant principles in the tort of negligence. It will then expound the aspects of autonomous vehicles, including their design and construction, which have raised issues requiring regulatory oversight. It will focus on the vehicles manufactured by Tesla and vehicles

---

[1]   Australian Consumer Law set out in Schedule 2 of the Competition and Consumer Act 2010 (Cth).

being tested by Uber as these have been involved in public harm of significant magnitude in the English-speaking world.

3.1.   LAW OF NEGLIGENCE

In discussing the regulation or governance of autonomous vehicles, one of the first areas that will give guidance is the law of torts, in particular, negligence law. Examining negligence law may be a useful first point of reference, for the standards set out in negligence law are intended to prevent harm and to assist in right conduct. For policy makers and regulators, the law of negligence will also guide them in directing their minds to the relevant and necessary legal and technological issues in setting out baseline standards before allowing the testing or the full deployment of autonomous or semi-autonomous vehicles on public roads.

Whilst each jurisdiction has its own intricate laws on negligence, generally speaking, before an act or omission can be classified as negligent in many jurisdictions, there must be:

1. a duty of care owed to the plaintiff by the defendant;
2. a breach of this duty of care by the defendant; and
3. recoverable damage caused to the plaintiff by the breach.

The discussion in this chapter is focused on expounding the relevant principles for the regulation of autonomous vehicles; hence, the issue of tortious damage caused by the breach necessary for a successful action in negligence will not be considered here.

3.1.1.   Duty of Care

The seminal case in establishing whether a duty of care exists in the tort of negligence is the UK case of *Donoghue v Stevenson*[2] where Lord Atkin laid down his 'neighbour principle'. Lord Atkin's formulation was that a defendant must avoid acts or omissions that will foreseeably harm persons who are so closely and directly affected by his acts or omissions that he ought reasonably to have them in contemplation as being so affected.[3] In the decades since, courts in the UK and other jurisdictions have developed more complex tests but the neighbour principle and the key element of foreseeability remain at the core of the duty.

---

[2]   [1932] AC 562.
[3]   Ibid, 580.

Donoghue v Stevenson[4] itself established that there was a duty of care owed by the manufacturer of a product to its consumers that the product be safe and fit for its purpose, and this remains good law in the UK today. Similarly in Australia, it is well settled that a broad duty of care is owed by a manufacturer and the common law provides that the manufacturer ought reasonably to have the user in contemplation when considering issues of design, manufacture and safety. There have been recent reforms in some of the states and territories in Australia to partially codify the law of negligence, but these do not affect the imposition of a duty of care on manufacturers with regard to the safety and fitness for purpose of the product.[5]

In the US, there is also no question that manufacturers owe a duty of care to ensure their creations are safe for normal use.[6] Similarly, in New Zealand, the New Zealand Supreme Court recently re-affirmed that the designer, manufacturer and supplier of building products owe a duty of care to the end user that the product is safe and fit for the purpose.[7]

In Singapore, for a duty of care to arise, the two-stage test laid down in *Spandeck Engineering (S) Pte Ltd v Defence Science & Technology Agency*[8] ('*Spandeck*') of proximity and policy with a preliminary requirement of factual foreseeability must be satisfied. Where the preliminary question of factual foreseeability and the first stage of the legal proximity test have been satisfied, a *prima facie* duty of care arises. At the second stage of the *Spandeck* test, policy considerations should be applied to the factual matrix to determine whether or not to negate this duty.[9] For the manufacturers of autonomous vehicles, there is little doubt that the preliminary requirement of factual foreseeability would be satisfied, for it is factually foreseeable that, should manufacturers be at fault in their design or manufacture of the autonomous vehicle, the owner or user or other road users will suffer loss and very likely personal injury as well. The first stage of the legal proximity test will also be satisfied as there is a physical and causal closeness between the manufacturer and the autonomous vehicle user, owner and other road users by the very fact that the autonomous vehicle will be travelling on public roads, open to all. Lastly, there

---

   [4]   [1932] AC 562.
   [5]   See for example South Australia's Civil Liability Act 1936 (SA).
   [6]   For a recent case involving manufacturer of technological products, see *Glorvigen v Cirrus Design Corp.*, 796 N.W.2d 541 (Minn. App. 2011).
   [7]   *Carter Holt Harvey Ltd v Minister of Education & Ors* [2015] NZCA 321 and *Carter Holt Harvey Limited v Minister of Education* [2016] NZSC 95.
   [8]   *Spandeck Engineering (S) Pte Ltd v Defence Science & Technology Agency* [2007] 4 SLR(R) 100 (CA).
   [9]   *Spandeck Engineering (S) Pte Ltd v Defence Science & Technology Agency* [2007] 4 SLR(R) 100 (CA), [83].

would appear to be no policy reasons that would serve to negate the liability of the autonomous vehicle manufacturer at this point in time.

It is not difficult to understand why most jurisdictions would impose a duty of care on manufacturers that their creations are safe and fit for the purposes they were created. Other than product liability laws which may be complex, this is the basic way to ensure citizens are kept safe from malfunctioning and exploding devices in their everyday lives.

3.1.2. Breach of Duty of Care

The second element required for the tort of negligence is a breach of the duty of care. The exact formulation for a breach of the duty of care may vary from jurisdiction to jurisdiction, but the core question is whether the defendant has failed to meet an appropriate standard, usually stated as the standard of the reasonable person placed in the same circumstances. In the case of autonomous vehicle manufacturers, the standard will be what the reasonable professional manufacturer of vehicles would do in the same situation.

At its core, the reasonable person would take reasonable care, hence the inquiry becomes whether reasonable care has been taken by the defendant to avoid causing reasonably foreseeable harm. This formulation is, of course, a very general one and may not fully describe the complex requirements for breach of duty in, for example, medical negligence cases.[10] However, for the purposes here of elucidating the guiding principles for a regulatory framework for the manufacturers of autonomous vehicles, it provides an adequate and workable baseline.

3.2. CHOICE AND NUMBER OF DEVICES/SYSTEMS IN AUTONOMOUS VEHICLES

For an autonomous vehicle manufacturer to take reasonable care in developing a usable and safe autonomous vehicle, the baseline standard is that the autonomous vehicle must be able to drive and adequately detect and avoid all kinds of obstacles, whether they be humans, animals or inanimate objects. This surely must be the basic requirement to meet the duty of care for a device that claims to be able to drive itself.

As Chapter 2 has elucidated, there is no 'one-sensor-does-everything' for autonomous vehicles – what is required for an effective autonomous vehicle is

---

[10] See for example, *Bolam v Friern Hospital Management Committee* [1957] 1 WLR 582 and *Bolitho v City and Hackney Health Authority* [1998] AC 232 in the UK.

the fusion of multiple sensors together into a sensor suite to complement each other.

The first task for any developer of autonomous vehicles is to assemble all of the relevant sensors and devices and determine if the sum of the devices does indeed adequately detect all possible objects and obstacles. The strengths and weaknesses of each of the sensors need to be taken into account and weighed up to see how best they can be used to complement each other.

The limitations of the different types of sensors are fairly well understood and the usual practice by autonomous vehicle developers is to construct suites of complementary sensors that are positioned all around the vehicle. Sensors need to be placed all around the vehicle to ensure that there are no blind spots, whether the blind spots are due to occluded views (visual blind spot) or the inability of sensors to detect certain kinds of obstructions or objects made from certain kinds of material (material blind spots).[11]

The autonomous vehicle developer needs to ensure that the limitations of each type of sensor are compensated for in some way by other sensors or devices. Each type of sensor provides different kinds of data and may have limitations related to field of view, ambient operating conditions and the elements in the environment that it can sense.[12]

High-resolution lidars are not as effective in poor weather conditions such as rain, fog and snow. Radars do not suffer from poor weather conditions but they are not as accurate as lidars and provide less detailed information. In addition, importantly, they have difficulty in detecting humans and other non-metallic creatures. Cameras can detect colours of surfaces but they suffer in conditions of bright sunlight, glare, sudden change in lighting conditions and nighttime conditions. GPS systems may give some idea of the position of the autonomous vehicle but generally GPS systems have an error of several metres, so that they cannot be entirely relied on for localization; instead, pre-built three-dimensional HD maps of the surrounding areas are essential in the localization process.[13]

From just this summary of characteristics, it is clear that for an autonomous vehicle to be able to drive and adequately detect all kinds of obstacles, whether they be humans, animals or inanimate objects, the autonomous vehicle must have on-board multiple redundant overlapping detection systems.[14] The systems must overlap to ensure there are no blind spots at all and there must

---

[11] James M Anderson et al, *Autonomous Vehicle Technology: A Guide for Policymakers* (Rand Corp 2016), 63.

[12] Ibid.

[13] See generally Chapter 2.

[14] See also Devin Coldewey, 'Here's how Uber's self-driving cars are supposed to detect pedestrians', *TechCrunch* (20 March 2018) <https://techcrunch.com/2018/03/

be multiple redundant systems in the event that one or more of the systems malfunction or fail. Having multiple redundant systems also enables the autonomous vehicle to sense the surrounding environment better when it combines the data collected from the different devices. For example, a camera can detect the colour of surfaces in the distance while lidar can be used to determine the material as that surface approaches; when integrated, a system can learn that green surfaces in the distance correspond to grass, enabling the autonomous vehicle to have a better sense of the environment that is far away.

For an autonomous vehicle manufacturer to meet this standard of care, it must ensure that the autonomous vehicle has on-board a number of essential devices. Whilst it is true that, in time, there may be technological advancements which might be able to better perform the tasks undertaken by the list of devices highlighted below, until such a time, should an autonomous vehicle manufacturer omit any of the devices listed below, the manufacturer must be able to show how the missing device or devices can be technically compensated for by its configuration of on-board devices. It would be wise for a governmental experts panel to assess such claims before allowing the trial of autonomous vehicles on public roads. Should the autonomous vehicle manufacturer raise claims of trade secrets and refuse such an assessment, then it should not be allowed to test its autonomous vehicles on public roads and perhaps should conduct testing within closed circuits. Some may argue that this is a draconian approach that inhibits innovation; however, such arguments are misplaced and do not give due weight to the duty or responsibility that governments have to protect their citizens. After all, would any government allow the live testing of ammunitions and firearms in a public place accessible by all?

It must be stressed that the following list is not a static list but it is a list that is relatively stable given the current state of technology and bearing in mind that any new technological developments will take at least a few years of testing and refinement.

3.2.1.   GPS Systems

GPS systems provide information about one of the core issues involved in driving, namely, the vehicle's current position, such as which street it is on, if it is on a street, and which lane. This is essential information for an autonomous vehicle as one of the main functions of a vehicle is to travel and remain on the road and not venture into curbs, gutters, rivers, drains, signs, buildings and so on. However, current GPS systems can only provide location information

---

19/heres-how-ubers-self-driving-cars-are-supposed-to-detect-pedestrians/>   accessed 23 April 2018.

down to around 4 or 5 metres.[15] Further, the reception of signals to and from satellites may be hindered owing to the terrain and the GPS system may be completely off line.

To counter GPS systems' inability to give precise location information, GPS systems on autonomous vehicles must be complemented by HD maps.

3.2.2. High-definition Maps

HD maps have become part of the suite of essential equipment for autonomous vehicles. They enable the autonomous vehicle to pinpoint the vehicle's exact location. An autonomous vehicle can compare its current surroundings with the surroundings captured in the HD maps.[16] This is the only way it can pinpoint its exact location as the autonomous vehicle has no other reference points to help it determine its location given that GPS coordinates are generally only accurate to 4 or 5 metres.

The more accurate and clear the HD map is, the more easy it will be for the autonomous vehicle to determine its exact location. The limitation with HD maps is that, if the surrounding environment changes, such as road works, road diversions or a new signalized traffic junction is created, then the autonomous vehicle will not be able to accurately and confidently pinpoint its exact location. If this occurs in only some situations, it may or may not be critical to an autonomous vehicle depending on how the manufacturer has designed the system to react when this happens. It may be something that the manufacturers have pre-programmed into the system, or it may have been left to an AI system.

From the foregoing, it should be evident that, not only should an autonomous vehicle utilize HD maps, but that the HD maps should be relatively up to date and accurate with adequate resolution.

3.2.3. Lidars

For an autonomous vehicle to be able to even utilize the HD maps at all, it must necessarily have on-board lidars to construct three-dimensional maps of the vehicle's current surroundings and compare the three-dimensional maps with the HD maps.[17] There should be sufficient lidars on the autonomous vehicle to

---

[15] Erico Guizzo, 'How Google's self-driving car works', *IEEE Spectrum* (18 October 2011) <https://spectrum.ieee.org/automaton/robotics/artificial-intelligence/how-google-self-driving-car-works> accessed 23 April 2018.

[16] Ibid.

[17] Ibid. See also Alex Davies, 'What is Lidar, why do self-driving cars need it, and can it see nerf bullets?' *Wired* (6 February 2018) <https://www.wired.com/story/lidar-self-driving-cars-luminar-video/> accessed 21 April 2018.

capture the full 360 degrees around the autonomous vehicle, upward facing as well as downward facing. There should be no blind spots.

In Waymo's fact sheet of its lidar system on its autonomous vehicles,[18] it states that its self-driving Pacifica minivan has three types of lidars. It claims that two of these three sensors are completely new categories of lidars, designed and built by Waymo. The two new lidars have yet to be independently assessed but the functions of the lidar system on Waymo's autonomous vehicles are reported as follows:

- *Short-range lidar:* Waymo's new type of lidar positioned to give the autonomous vehicle an uninterrupted surround view, downwards, behind and next to the vehicle's body, so the vehicle can detect small humans and objects.
- *Long-range lidar:* Waymo's new type of lidar that claims to understand subtle signals such as hand gestures from far away. It reportedly works with the primary lidar to quickly zoom 360 degrees around the car and can detect incredibly small details, such as a cyclist waving to let the autonomous vehicle pass 220 metres, or two football fields, away, while driving at full speed. If indeed the lidar has such a long range, then it is a huge technological improvement as the average range was previously around 120 metres.
- *High-resolution lidar:* this appears to be the normal lidar but when coupled with the short- and long-range lidars, this high-resolution lidar assists in the creation of the HD maps.

Irrespective of Waymo's self-proclaimed superior lidars, all autonomous vehicles must have sufficient and appropriately positioned lidars all around their vehicles to achieve a full 360 degrees view all around the autonomous vehicle. Traditional rotating lidars mounted on the rooftop of autonomous vehicles do have 360 degree view but the newer solid-state lidars tend to have a reduced field of view of about 120 degrees.[19] For the solid-state lidars to achieve a 360 degree field of view, many sensors must be utilized and integrated. Some have opined that four to six lidars would be required;[20] however, this does not seem to be an accurate calculation. Indeed, it appears to assume that the autonomous

---

[18] The information in this and the next three paragraphs on Waymo's lidar system is from Waymo, 'Fact Sheet: LiDAR, the "eyes" of our self-driving car' <https://storage .googleapis.com/sdc-prod/v1/press/Waymo_Lidar_Fact_Sheet.pdf> accessed 21 April 2018.

[19] John R Quain, 'What self-driving cars see', *The New York Times* (25 May 2017) <https://www.nytimes.com/2017/05/25/automobiles/wheels/lidar-self-driving-cars .html> accessed 21 April 2018.

[20] Ibid.

vehicle is just a single dot that has 360 degrees around it. Unfortunately, this is not the case as even a lidar mounted on the roof of a vehicle may not have a field of view down the lower sides of the vehicle. An autonomous vehicle is large and has four sides to it with four corners. If a solid-state lidar has only 120 degrees field of view, to achieve a full view at each corner, two lidars would be required, and with four corners of an autonomous vehicle, the minimum number of solid-state lidars would be eight.[21]

Solid-state lidars do have the advantage that they are smaller and, importantly, they eliminate moving parts involved in the optical mechanisms, which may enable their mass manufacture, thereby bringing manufacturing costs down.

Lidars are also useful for detecting and tracking humans, animals, objects and obstacles with great precision.[22] In fact, given that lidars are the only technology currently available that can detect and measure the distance to objects with high accuracy and precision, this is another reason why they are an essential piece of hardware for autonomous vehicles. In addition, lidars are able to function in all lighting conditions, both during the day and at night; hence they are also essential to the 'night vision' package of an autonomous vehicle.

The main limitation of lidars is that they currently can only detect with accuracy up to a range of around 120 metres,[23] which does not give the autonomous vehicle a lot of warning about objects beyond the 120 metres range. To overcome this limitation, lidars must work hand-in-hand with radars, which have a much longer range of detection.

3.2.4.   Radars

Radars have a much greater detection range compared with lidars and can detect objects 200 metres away.[24] This is essential because as the autonomous vehicle is continuously moving, early warning of objects, especially fast-moving objects headed towards it, is crucial for it to be able to properly respond to the situation.

Radars complement lidars both in the shorter range and in the longer range. Readings from the shorter range can confirm the readings from lidars. Readings in the longer range can be passed on for lidars to be on alert when the objects come within range. The ability of lidars to calculate precisely and

---

[21]   This based on the author's own calculations.
[22]   John R Quain (n 19).
[23]   James M Anderson et al (n 11), 61-62.
[24]   Ryan Whitwam, 'How Google's self-driving cars detect and avoid obstacles', *Extremetech* (8 September 2014) <http://www.extremetech.com/extreme/189486 -howgoogles-self-driving-cars-detect-and-avoid-obstacles> accessed 23 April 2018.

accurately the distance of objects can assist the autonomous vehicle in making a decision of whether to swerve or to apply the brakes, or both.

Radars work well on metallic objects; they are thus effective in detecting other vehicles and their speed, road signs, traffic signals and metal barriers amongst other items.[25] For this reason, they are also essential equipment on autonomous vehicles. Further, there must be sufficient radars placed all around the autonomous vehicle to ensure that every single direction is captured by the radars, including upward and downward facing.

For autonomous vehicles that are trucks, radars are even more crucial as trucks and other heavy vehicles require more time and distance to come to a stop than a passenger car. Longer-range sensors are needed to fully understand the environment. Lidars, with their shorter range, are reportedly not used by autonomous trucking technology company TuSimple because of the high cost of lidars and the perception that the rotating parts of lidars are not reliable.[26] This view appears to stem from a business decision and not one that is necessarily ethical. Further, it appears to be an untenable position as Waymo reported in January 2017 that it had pushed down the pricing of lidars by 90 per cent.[27] A single top-of-the-range lidar used to cost around $75,000 when they were produced almost exclusively by Velodyne, a Silicon Valley-based technology company. Since December 2015, Waymo (or its parent Alphabet) has been producing lidars, which has reportedly helped the company cut down its production costs.[28]

Vehicles that have radars fitted at the front and back of vehicles have been on the market for some time. They are often part of a system called adaptive cruise control (ACC). ACC is an intelligent form of cruise control that slows down and speeds up automatically to keep pace with the vehicle in front.[29]

---

[25] Jamie Condliffe, 'This image is why self-driving cars come loaded with many types of sensors', *MIT Technology Review* (21 July 2017) <https://www.technologyreview.com/s/608321/this-image-is-why-self-driving-cars-come-loaded-with-many-types-of-sensors/> accessed 23 April 2018.

[26] Eric Brandt, 'Lidar vs Radar: Pros and cons of different autonomous driving technologies', *The Drive* (12 December 2017) <http://www.thedrive.com/sheetmetal/16916/lidar-vs-radar-pros-and-cons-of-different-autonomous-driving-technologies> accessed 23 April 2018. The company spokesman said '[w]e're trying to hit a commercial price point that is practical and you can't do that with lidar'.

[27] Christian Gilbertsen, 'Google's self-driving car arm Waymo cuts lidar prices by 90 percent', *The Drive* (9 January 2017) <http://www.thedrive.com/news/6863/googles-self-driving-car-arm-waymo-cuts-lidar-prices-by-90-percent?iid=sr-link9> accessed 23 April 2018.

[28] Ibid.

[29] Bill Howard, 'What is adaptive cruise control, and how does it work?', *Extremetech* (4 June 2013) <https://www.extremetech.com/extreme/157172-what-is-adaptive-cruise-control-and-how-does-it-work> accessed 23 April 2018.

Drivers find it helpful during peak hour traffic where the traffic is often continuously stop and go. ACC is often coupled with a forward collision warning
system, which will apply the brakes for the driver if the radar calculates that
the vehicle is likely to crash into the vehicle in front. This is yet another reason
why radars are a must in any autonomous vehicle – even under normal driving
conditions, radars do prevent collisions from occurring. Radar systems on
autonomous vehicles, however, should be slightly more sophisticated than the
ones utilized for ACC, which are built for narrower purposes.

3.2.5.   Cameras

At present, the only device that can distinguish between colours is the camera,
whether it be a video or still camera; hence autonomous vehicles require a suite
of cameras with adequate image resolution to continuously capture images.
Of course the suite of cameras must be coupled with sound algorithms and
software to determine the colour of an object and the accuracy is only as good
as the software.[30] Nevertheless, cameras are currently the only device that can
determine whether a traffic light is red or green, detect a red Stop sign, detect
whether the vehicle in front has suddenly braked because its red brake lights
have suddenly lit up, see pedestrians crossing and generally read road signs.

Lidars and radars can determine shapes of objects but they cannot give
meaning to colour; hence optical cameras with sophisticated computer vision
algorithms are essential to assist the autonomous vehicle in interpreting the
surfaces of some key objects found on roads. To ensure a comprehensive view
of the surroundings, there needs to be multiple cameras of different types
attached to the autonomous vehicle positioned at appropriate locations covering multiple angles. Waymo's vehicles have many cameras around the exterior
of the vehicle in pairs with a small separation between them.[31] The pairing of
the cameras in this way creates a parallax because of the overlapping fields of
view, and like human eyes, allows the system to track an object's distance in
real time.[32] Once an object has been detected by more than one camera, the
vehicle can calculate the location of the object. Waymo's cameras have a 50
degree field of view and are accurate up to about 30 metres.[33]

Whilst cameras can interpret some of their surroundings through the colours
they can perceive, cameras have their own limitations, such as in low light or
at nighttime, glare, rain, fog, snow and where there are shadows.

---

[30]   Devin Coldewey (n 14).
[31]   Ryan Whitwam (n 24).
[32]   Ibid.
[33]   Ibid.

3.2.6.   Infrared Systems

For an autonomous vehicle to be able to function at nighttime, it must include infrared systems. Whilst radars can function at nighttime, radars are best at detecting metallic objects and have difficulty detecting humans; hence infrared systems are required to detect humans and animals at nighttime. It is true that lidars can detect humans at night but bearing in mind that for an autonomous vehicle manufacturer to meet the standard of taking reasonable care in developing a usable and safe autonomous vehicle, it must have on-board multiple redundant overlapping detection systems.[34] This would require the presence of the infrared system as a back-up to the lidar system in detecting living creatures.

Infrared systems are also unaffected by direct sunlight and abrupt lighting changes, such as when entering or exiting a tunnel. Nor do they require clear visibility to function, thus, they would, to a certain extent, take over the role of cameras, which are inadequate in these scenarios.[35]

3.2.7.   Summary of Required Standard of Care for Systems

This section has expounded that for an autonomous vehicle manufacturer to meet the standard of taking reasonable care in developing a usable and safe autonomous vehicle, the autonomous vehicle must be able to drive and adequately detect and avoid all kinds of obstacles, whether they be humans, animals or inanimate objects. This means that the required standard of care is that the autonomous vehicle must have on-board multiple redundant overlapping detection systems. The essential systems that have been presented above are: GPS systems, HD maps, lidars, radars, cameras and infrared systems. There must of course be sufficient numbers of these devices and they must be appropriately positioned on the autonomous vehicle. It would still amount to a breach of duty of care if, for example, an insufficient number of devices were deployed or if they were not appropriately positioned. This is because the aim is to always capture a clear 360 degrees view of the surrounding environment using all of these devices.

In addition to these baseline devices, many autonomous vehicles do have on-board other types of devices, such as sonar systems and ultrasonic sensors. These are to be encouraged as they do complement the work of lidars and

---

[34]   See Section 3.2 above.

[35]   Mark Harris, 'Night vision for self-driving cars', *IEEE Spectrum* (18 October 2017)   <https://spectrum.ieee.org/cars-that-think/transportation/self-driving/do-self driving-cars-need-night-vision> accessed 23 April 2018.

radars but on their own, their uses may be limited to short ranges. For example, the range of ultrasonic sensors is from 1 to 10 metres[36] and sonar is limited to 6 metres.[37] Developers of autonomous vehicles can of course utilize ultrasonic sensors and sonars as a last resort signal to trigger safety devices such as pre-tensioning the seatbelts, in addition to swerving or applying the brakes, as the object will be very close if it is detected by ultrasonic sensors or sonars.

It is almost a given but, for clarity, it must be articulated here that autonomous vehicles should, as a matter of back-up safety, include some basic driver controls in the autonomous vehicle, such as a steering wheel and brake pedals, even if they are Level 5 full automation vehicles. This is a basic standard of care owed to those inside the autonomous vehicle as well as pedestrians and other drivers. In the event of any malfunction, hacking or cybersecurity breach, a human being must be able to steer or brake or take other appropriate actions. This is even more critical in recent years where terrorists have utilized motor vehicles as a way of committing murder of innocent civilians. The technology for autonomous vehicles is not yet ripe and, even if it was mature, these basic safety driver controls are a necessity to protect all road users.

There have been some studies that have shown that humans are seemingly incapable of resuming control of a Level 3 vehicle quickly and take an average of 3–7 seconds, and as long as 10 seconds, to take control. As such, one scholar has suggested that these systems that allow humans to override are ineffective and unnecessary.[38] This kind of argument is simply untenable in the age of terrorism by ramming civilians with motor vehicles. If these basic driver controls are present, at least humans can take over and stop or swerve the vehicle to minimize the harm, even if it takes 10 seconds.

It is unfortunate that, at the time of writing, a battle is raging in the US Senate over a bill that, if passed, would allow masses of autonomous vehicles without such typical driver controls onto the public roads.[39] Consumer advocates have highlighted many loopholes in the bill, including the forced arbitration, which

---

[36]   Bing Shun Lim, Sye Loong Keoh and Vrizlynn L L Thing, 'Autonomous vehicle ultrasonic sensor vulnerability and impact assessment', IEEE World Forum on Internet of Things (WF-IoT) 2018, A*STAR Open Access Repository <http://oar.a-star.edu.sg:80/jspui/handle/123456789/2321> accessed 23 April 2018.

[37]   Ryan Whitwam (n 24).

[38]   Tracy Pearl, 'Fast and Furious: The misregulation of driverless cars' (2017) 73 NYU Annual Survey of American Law 19.

[39]   Keith Laing, 'Self-driving bill faces unclear path in Senate', *Detroit News* (23 April 2018) <https://www.detroitnews.com/story/business/autos/mobility/2018/04/23/self-driving-bill/34154717/> accessed 27 April 2018.

would prevent victims from commencing legal actions against the autonomous vehicle manufacturers. It remains to be seen how the battle will be fought out.[40]

With the standard of care for the choice and number of devices for autonomous vehicles set out, the following sections will turn to the well-reported accidents which have involved semi-autonomous vehicles and autonomous vehicles in the US and in China. The aim of considering these accidents is to test whether there may have been breaches in the required standard of care, and if there were, then they would provide guidance as to what kind of regulations or baseline standards would be appropriate.

3.3. THE STANDARD OF CARE FOR SYSTEMS – TESLA MODEL S 2016 ACCIDENT

The first fatality in the US involving a semi-autonomous vehicle was in May 2016 in a vehicle manufactured by Tesla, the Tesla Model S. The vehicle itself was not a fully autonomous vehicle but would be classified as Level 2 automation according to the Society of Automotive Engineers International classification. However, the accident did involve Telsa's much advertised Autopilot automated driving feature, which the company claimed could steer, detect obstacles and lane markings, drive, use the brakes, change lanes and manage speed during highway driving, not to mention self-parallel park and self-park in perpendicular positions.[41]

The Autopilot name of the feature is a misnomer. It suggests that no human intervention is needed, but at the same time, Tesla has also been maintaining that drivers must be constantly ready to take over from the vehicle's software system. Many, including, Germany's Federal Motor Transport Authority, have criticized Tesla for promoting the convenience of Autopilot as it misleads the drivers into thinking and trusting that the vehicle's software will be a competent driver.[42] Indeed, the Chief Executive Officer of Tesla, Elon Musk, publicly

---

[40] Amy Martyn, 'Despite pedestrian death, self-driving car industry lobbies for fast expansion of testing', *ConsumerAffairs* (29 March 2018) <https://www.consumeraffairs.com/news/despite-pedestrian-death-self-driving-car-industry-lobbies-for-fast-expansion-of-testing-032918.html> accessed 27 April 2018.

[41] Tesla's Autopilot website <https://www.tesla.com/autopilot/> accessed 23 April 2018.

[42] Germany's Federal Motor Transport Authority wrote to Tesla to demand that the misleading term 'Autopilot' be no longer used in advertising the system 'KBA: Tesla soll nicht mehr mit Begriff 'Autopilot' werben', *Bild am Sonntag* (16 October 2016) <https://www.bild.de/geld/aktuelles/wirtschaft/kba-tesla-soll-nicht-mehr-mit-begriff-autopilot-48311800.bild.html> accessed 23 April 2018. See also Tom Simonite, 'Fatal Tesla Autopilot crash is a reminder autonomous cars will sometimes screw up', *MIT Technology Review* (30 June 2016) <https://www.technologyreview.com/s/601822/

stated his company's data suggested that the Autopilot feature was twice as safe as human drivers.[43] However, at the time of the accident, rival company Google stated that its own experiments had shown that humans cannot be relied upon to be constantly ready to take over from the vehicle's software because humans quickly come to trust that the vehicle is competent at driving itself.[44]

On 7 May 2016, while the Autopilot feature was in control of the vehicle, a Tesla Model S sedan drove into an 18-wheel truck that was turning left in front of it at an intersection on a highway in Williston, Florida.[45] The semi-autonomous vehicle's brakes were not applied by the Tesla's Autopilot feature or the driver. The impact ripped off the roof of the Tesla Model S as it went under the truck. The owner and driver of the vehicle, Joshua Brown, was pronounced dead at the scene of the accident.[46]

There are two issues that need to be addressed regarding the standard of care owed by Tesla to the drivers of its vehicles. The first is the issue of requiring hands on the steering wheel; the second is the issue of the non-detection of the truck by the Tesla Model S sedan.

3.3.1.   Hands on Steering Wheel

In June 2017, the National Transportation Safety Board (NTSB) published the factual findings of its investigation.[47] Brown had been using the Autopilot feature as if it were a fully autonomous driving system. Of the 37 minutes that Brown had been using the Autopilot feature, he had placed his hands on the wheel for a total of only 25 seconds, despite seven separate visual warnings from the system, which flashed the message: Hold Steering Wheel.[48]

---

fatal-tesla-autopilot-crash-is-a-reminder-autonomous-cars-will-sometimes-screw-up/> accessed 23 April 2018.

[43]   Ibid.

[44]   Tom Simonite, 'Lazy humans shaped Google's new autonomous car', *MIT Technology Review* (30 May 2014) <https://www.technologyreview.com/s/527756/lazy-humans-shaped-googles-new-autonomous-car/> accessed 23 April 2018.

[45]   National Transportation Safety Board (NTSB), 'NTSB Opens Docket on Tesla Crash', *NTSB News Release* (19 June 2017) <https://www.ntsb.gov/news/press-releases/Pages/PR20170619.aspx> accessed 23 April 2018.

[46]   Ibid.

[47]   NTSB, *Docket & Docket Items* (15 June 2017) <https://go.usa.gov/xNvaE> accessed 23 April 2018.

[48]   NTSB Docket Management System, 'Errata – HP supplemental report – Driver assistance systems' (22 June 2017) <https://dms.ntsb.gov/pubdms/search/document.cfm?docID=453567&docketID=59989&mkey=93548> accessed 23 April 2018.

In a blog post, Tesla stated:[49]

It is important to note that Tesla disables Autopilot by default and requires explicit acknowledgement that the system is new technology and still in a public beta phase before it can be enabled. When drivers activate Autopilot, the acknowledgment box explains, among other things, that Autopilot 'is an assist feature that requires you to keep your hands on the steering wheel at all times,' and that 'you need to maintain control and responsibility for your vehicle' while using it. Additionally, every time that Autopilot is engaged, the car reminds the driver to 'Always keep your hands on the wheel. Be prepared to take over at any time.' The system also makes frequent checks to ensure that the driver's hands remain on the wheel and provides visual and audible alerts if hands-on is not detected. It then gradually slows down the car until hands-on is detected again.

In short, Tesla was stressing that the Autopilot feature is only a safety mechanism and it was disclaiming liability as the terms and conditions of the proper use of the vehicle required Brown to have kept his hands on the wheel, which Brown failed to do.

Importantly, in the extract above of the blog post, Tesla claimed that the vehicle will check for the driver's hands on the steering wheel and it will slow down until hands-on is detected again. At the time of the crash, the vehicle was travelling at 74 miles per hour or nearly 120 kilometres an hour, which is a very high speed. Brown had been using the Autopilot feature for 37 minutes and his hands were only on the wheel for just 25 seconds.

In the NTSB's factual findings, it stated that:[50]

During the time when TACC and Autosteer were active, the system presented a visual warning to the driver on 7 occasions (bar presented in the instrument panel that reads 'Hold Steering Wheel'). On 6 occasions, the visual warnings occasions were followed with the initial level of auditory warning. The second level of auditory warning did not occur during the last ignition cycle, nor did the system initiate Autosteer disengagement protocol.

From the factual findings, there was no trigger of the disengagement of the Autosteer protocol, which would have slowed the vehicle down and brought it to a stop.

---

[49] Tesla website blog post, 'A tragic loss' (30 June 2016) <https://www.tesla.com/blog/tragic-loss?utm_campaign=Blog_063016&utm_source=Twitter&utm_medium=social> accessed 23 April 2018.

[50] NTSB Docket Management System (n 48).

The NTSB released its report on the accident in September 2017.[51] In its report, the NTSB explained that, for the vehicle to come to a complete stop, it would require an 'incapacitated or completely unresponsive driver'.[52] The reason for this is because the Autopilot feature uses a series of warnings to encourage the driver to interact with the steering wheel.[53] The first of these is a visual warning, which appears in the instrument panel display. To satisfy the system, the driver needs to apply only a little torque on the steering wheel, and the system will leave the driver alone. If the system does not detect any hands on the wheel after this visual warning, it will sound an auditory chime. If it still does not detect any hands on the steering wheel, it sounds a second, louder chime. If the driver still does not touch the steering wheel, the system presents a final visual warning in the instrument panel display. If the driver still does not put their hands on the steering wheel, then the Autopilot feature decelerates the Tesla to a full stop in the current lane and activates the vehicle's hazard flashers.[54]

It must be questioned whether such a series of warnings coupled with applying only a little torque on the steering wheel is an effective mechanism to ensure that the driver uses the Autopilot system as a safety mechanism only and not an autonomous vehicle system, especially since it is easy to cheat a torque sensor with an orange or a bottle jammed in the inner circle of the steering wheel. The opinion of the NTSB report seems to suggest that it is not. The report said:[55]

> driving is a highly visual task, so the driver's touching the steering wheel may not accurately indicate that he or she is fully engaged with the driving task. Simply checking whether the driver has placed a hand on the steering wheel gives little indication of where the driver is focusing his or her attention. The NTSB concludes that because driving is an inherently visual task and a driver may touch the steering wheel without visually assessing the roadway, traffic conditions, or vehicle control system performance, monitoring steering wheel torque provides a poor surrogate means of determining the automated vehicle driver's degree of engagement with the driving task.

---

[51]   NTSB, 'Accident report: Collision between a car operating with automated vehicle control systems and a tractor-semitrailer truck near Williston, Florida May 7, 2016' (12 September 2017) <https://www.ntsb.gov/investigations/AccidentReports/Reports/HAR1702.pdf> accessed 5 May 2018.
[52]   Ibid, 11.
[53]   Ibid.
[54]   Ibid.
[55]   NTSB (n 51), 34–35.

From this assessment that the hands-on-steering-wheel check was a 'poor' means of ensuring drivers perform the driving task, it would appear that the use of this check was inappropriate and very likely to amount to a breach of the duty of care owed by Tesla for a Level 2 vehicle to the drivers.

Furthermore, the report went on and commented that much substantial naturalistic driving research has been conducted on on-road driver behaviour. It cited one study by car manufacturer Volvo in Sweden and two such studies by the Virginia Tech Transportation Institute (VTTI). One study has been concluded by VTTI in 2005 and another is currently in progress concerning the use of vehicles with Level 2 automation capabilities from five different car manufacturers. The report stated that data from both forward- and driver-facing cameras have been collected to better understand driver behaviour and that such studies are essential to understanding drivers' interactions with automated systems and the extent to which they may misuse them. Nevertheless, the report pointed out that these studies have also analysed different approaches to system monitoring, such as the use of eye-tracking cameras, which have long been used in driving simulation research. Indeed, Toyota has deployed an eye-tracking system on its Lexus brand vehicles, and Volvo has announced plans to use eye-tracking technology in its Driver State Estimation system. Further, the report highlighted that the Driver Attention System on the 2018 Cadillac CT6 Super Cruise vehicle uses a small infrared camera located at the top of the steering column with the camera focused exclusively on the driver and uses infrared light to track the driver's head position – should the driver look away or lean over, the system warnings will light up within seconds, followed by the system switching itself off if the driver does not pay attention to the road.[56]

From the foregoing, it is not difficult to surmise that eye-tracking or head position tracking technologies would be more appropriate and effective than Tesla's system of requiring the driver to momentarily touch the steering wheel, and these eye-tracking or head position tracking technologies would meet the standard of care required for a Level 2 vehicle manufacturer.

In addition to the issue of the use of the hands-on-steering-wheel check being inappropriate, the time duration set by Tesla before the warning alerts are triggered also reveal another shortcoming in the design of the system.

In the report, it was stated that the longest period between alerts during which Autopilot feature did not detect the driver's hands on the steering wheel was nearly 6 minutes.[57] In the chart shown of the entire 41 minutes journey,

---

[56] Ibid, 35.
[57] Ibid, 14.

the last 6 minutes was the longest interval where there were no hands on the steering wheel as well as no visual warning.[58]

The Autopilot feature was turned on at the 3 minute mark, visual warnings occurred at 9 minutes, just after 14 minutes, just before 18 minutes and at 21 minutes. Each of these visual warnings was followed by the driver touching the steering wheel, probably for only a few seconds. The Autopilot feature was switched off at 24 minutes for less than a minute, then the visual warnings came on again at just before 28 minutes, at 31 minutes and just after 34 minutes. Again, immediately after each of these visual warnings, Brown touched the steering wheel for probably only a few seconds. Brown switched off and on the Autopilot feature just after 34 minutes and the crash occurred at 41 minutes without any further visual warnings or hands on the steering wheel by Brown.[59]

From the series of warnings and the switching of the Autopilot feature on and off three times, it could have been that Brown was testing the system, perhaps even testing how long it would take before the vehicle would in fact slow down and come to a stop. The critical point to note is that, just before the crash, around 6 minutes or more had passed without Brown's hands being on the steering wheel and without any alert whatsoever. Six minutes is an extremely long time for the vehicle to be 'unattended' by the driver, especially at 74 miles per hour, and thus, it would not appear that the manufacturer had intended the Autopilot system to be used as a safety mechanism only rather than an autonomous vehicle system. If the Autopilot system really was intended to be used as a safety mechanism, then the deactivate function would be triggered in instances other than where the driver was an 'incapacitated or completely unresponsive driver' as the NTSB had put it.[60]

Indeed, the NTSB stated that the 'way that the Tesla Autopilot system monitored and responded to the driver's interaction with the steering wheel was not an effective method of ensuring driver engagement'.[61] The NTSB also made note that the United Nations Economic Commission for Europe had adopted a new regulation regarding the hands-off warning time in lane-keeping systems on vehicles. This regulation requires lane-keeping systems to provide an initial visual warning after 15 seconds of hands-off driving and to deactivate the lane-keeping function in a controlled manner after 1 minute of hands-off driving.[62] This is a far safer and more appropriate time interval than the more than 6 minutes that is programmed into the Tesla Model S.

---

[58]   Ibid, 15.
[59]   Ibid, 15.
[60]   Ibid, 11.
[61]   Ibid, 41.
[62]   Ibid, 35.

Lastly, the acknowledgement box referred to by Tesla in its blog post stated that the Autopilot feature 'is an assist feature that requires you to keep your hands on the steering wheel at all times'.[63] Allowing drivers to keep their hands away from the steering wheel for more than 6 minutes is hardly meeting this requirement of keeping your hands 'on the steering wheel at all times'. It seems quite clear that this time interval is a breach of the standard of care that Tesla, as the manufacturer of a Level 2 vehicle, owed to Brown, the driver. Tesla itself claimed that the vehicle required the driver to keep their hands on the steering wheel and that it would slow itself down if hands were not detected. Brown's hands were consistently not on the steering wheel, and for a continuous 6 minutes travelling at 74 miles per hour and the vehicle did not slow down. This would, in and of itself, be a breach of Tesla's standard of care owed towards the owner driver, not to mention a breach of a contractual term, subject to any valid exemption clauses.

The NTSB report on the accident concluded that the truck driver's failure to yield to Brown's oncoming Tesla combined with the Tesla driver's inattention to the task of driving and his overreliance on the Autopilot feature caused the accident.[64] On 2 May 2018, the NTSB released a statement that its investigation into the crash did not assess the 'effectiveness' of the Autopilot technology.[65] It is unclear why the NTSB did not concern itself with this issue as the Autopilot technology would appear to have been a substantial contributor to the accident – it was the use of the poor hands on steering wheel detection system and the long time intervals it was configured with that allowed Brown to not pay attention to the roads, as well as the truck driver not giving Brown the right of way that caused the accident. Although Brown's Tesla was travelling at 74 miles per hour and was over the speed limit of 65 miles per hour, the NTSB did not appear to think that this was a contributing factor.[66]

3.3.2.   Non-detection of the 18 Wheeler Truck

The second issue of the non-detection of the truck by the Tesla Model S sedan is an issue that is very important for fully autonomous vehicles. In a blog post just after the accident, Tesla stated that '[n]either Autopilot nor the driver

---

[63]   Tesla website blog post (n 49).

[64]   NTSB (n 51), 41–42.

[65]   David Shepardson, 'U.S. safety agency: Prior probe did not assess "effectiveness" of Tesla Autopilot', *Reuters* (3 May 2018) <https://www.reuters.com/article/tesla-autopilot/us-safety-agency-prior-probe-did-not-assess-effectiveness-of-tesla-autopilot-idUSL1N1S91XY> accessed 5 May 2018.

[66]   NTSB (n 51), 41–42.

noticed the white side of the tractor trailer against a brightly lit sky, so the brake was not applied'.[67] The NTSB report also stated:[68]

> The Tesla's automated vehicle control system was not designed to, and did not, identify the truck crossing the car's path or recognize the impending crash; consequently, the Autopilot system did not reduce the car's velocity, the forward collision warning system did not provide an alert, and the automatic emergency braking did not activate.

This conclusion by the NTSB that the automated vehicle control system was not designed to identify the truck crossing the car's path or recognize the impending crash seems puzzling. What the NTSB meant was that, in terms of the vehicle's classification, the 2015 Tesla Model S was not designed to do such things, not that the vehicle was technically not designed to do such things. There is quite a difference, especially since, although the Tesla Model S was designated as a Level 2 automation vehicle, all of the marketing for the vehicle and the way the vehicle was designed allowed drivers to treat the Tesla Model S for all intents and purposes as a vehicle with a much higher level of automation, possibly even a Level 4 vehicle.[69]

The NTSB explained:[70]

> Current Level 2 vehicle automation technologies cannot reliably identify and respond to crossing vehicle traffic. NHTSA's ODI report on the Tesla Models S and X, which was prompted by the Williston crash, states: 'None of the companies contacted by ODI indicated that AEB systems used in their products through MY 2016 production were designed to brake for crossing path collisions' .... As part of its defect investigation, NHTSA conducted a series of test-track-based AEB evaluations on the Tesla Model S, as well as a peer vehicle system. The testing confirmed that the Tesla AEB system avoided crashes for the majority of rear-end scenarios, and its TACC generally provided enough braking to avoid rear-end crash scenarios; but neither test vehicle effectively responded to 'target vehicles' in straight-crossing-path or left-turn-across-path scenarios. NHTSA concluded that there was no defect in the design of the Tesla crash avoidance and mitigation systems.

From this extracted paragraph, two things are clear. The first is that for Level 2 vehicle automation technologies, they cannot and are not expected to be able to identify and respond to crossing vehicle traffic. The Tesla Model S was a Level 2 vehicle and the accident involved a truck more or less crossing in its path. Along this line of reasoning, Tesla is absolved from any wrong doing, as

---

[67] Tesla website blog post (n 49).
[68] NTSB (n 51), 41.
[69] Tom Simonite (n 42).
[70] NTSB (n 51), 30–31.

far as the vehicle's classifications and capabilities are concerned. This line of reasoning is, however, extremely superficial for three reasons.

First, it ignores the fact this limitation of crossing vehicle traffic was not made known to drivers. Indeed, Tesla has 'promoted the technology as capable of handling almost all aspects of a car journey, adding to the impression that it is at the forefront of today's driverless car technology'.[71] On Tesla's website, it still claims 'All Tesla vehicles produced in our factory, including Model 3, have the hardware needed for full self-driving capability at a safety level substantially greater than that of a human driver'.[72] Statements such as these lull Tesla drivers into a false sense of security that their Tesla vehicles can drive themselves. Even the Tesla S Owner's Manual[73] dated 22 March 2018 does not really explicitly spell out this limitation. Under the heading of 'Forward Collision Warning', the Manual simply states: 'The forward looking camera(s) and the radar sensor monitor the area in front of Model S for the presence of an object such as a vehicle, bicycle, or pedestrian'.[74] There is no mention of it not being able to detect crossing objects. If anything, this sentence gives the general impression that the forward collision warning (FCW) is very adept at detecting any objects in front of the Tesla Model S.

Under 'Automatic Emergency Braking', the current 2018 Owner's Manual states:[75]

> The forward looking camera(s) and the radar sensor are designed to determine the distance from an object (vehicle, motorcycle, bicycle, or pedestrian) traveling in front of Model S. When a frontal collision is considered unavoidable, Automatic Emergency Braking is designed to apply the brakes to reduce the severity of the impact.

It is unclear if the 2016 version of the Tesla Model S Owner's Manual on Automatic Emergency Braking (AEB) also contained the sentence concerning objects travelling in front of the Tesla Model S. Even if it did, it is ambiguous in meaning: does the object have to be travelling in the exact same lane in front of the Tesla Model S? In any event, the presence of the earlier sentence on the FCW would give the impression that the vehicle would be able to detect

---

[71] Richard Waters, 'Tesla says crash car was running on autopilot', *Financial Times* (31 March 2018) <https://www.ft.com/content/aa8fdab8-34cd-11e8-8b98-2f31af407cc8> accessed 23 April 2018.

[72] Tesla website <https://www.tesla.com/autopilot> accessed 23 April 2018.

[73] Tesla website, *Tesla Model S Owner's Manual* <https://www.tesla.com/sites/default/files/model_s_owners_manual_north_america_en_us.pdf> accessed 23 April 2018.

[74] Ibid, 92.

[75] Ibid, 93.

crossing vehicles. However, according to the data taken from Brown's vehicle, there was no FCW alert.[76] This would already indicate a breach of the standard of care owed by Tesla. A manufacturer cannot claim that its vehicle is capable of certain functions when the vehicle clearly cannot without suffering legal ramifications such as negligence.

The second reason why the NTSB's statement is superficial is because it disregards the manufacturer's design choices (such as the hands-on-steering-wheel-for-a-few-seconds system), which allow the driver to treat the vehicle as if it is a fully autonomous Level 5 vehicle. Third, NTSB's statement also disregards the manufacturer's continued commendation of the 'convenience' of the Autopilot feature.[77] The Autopilot feature can only be described as 'convenient' if the driver is not really paying attention to the driving task; otherwise, the Autopilot feature is a feature that one would describe as 'safe'.

Turning to the second message from the extracted paragraph concerning current Level 2 vehicle automation technologies from the NTSB report,[78] it appears to suggest that, because subsequent crash tests by NHTSA showed that the Tesla and a peer vehicle both did not effectively respond to other vehicles in a straight-crossing-path or left-turn-across-path scenarios, there was no defect in the design of the Tesla crash avoidance and mitigation systems. This seems like a circular method of investigating defects in the design of the Tesla.

The following will raise two arguments why the Tesla Model S was poorly designed in its failure to detect the white-coloured truck and these two arguments, separately and combined, would again point to a breach of the standard of care owed by Tesla to the drivers of its vehicles.

The NTSB report noted that the Tesla Model S had both FCW and AEB systems using a camera and radar sensors and computer processing to provide warnings to the driver and to activate braking to prevent or mitigate an imminent crash.[79] The NTSB noted that the 'system is designed to recognize and detect slow, stopped, and decelerating vehicles when they are traveling ahead of the Tesla in the same lane'.[80] The NTSB does not explain how the system works, or why it is limited to only being able to detect vehicles when they are travelling ahead of the Tesla in the same lane.

The performance data recorded in Brown's vehicle showed no indication of an FCW or AEB event, or any other event that indicated the detection of a vehicle or an object at or just before the time of the crash.[81] Of course, without

---

76   NTSB (n 51), 30.
77   Tom Simonite (n 42).
78   See main text at footnote 70.
79   NTSB (n 51), 30.
80   Ibid.
81   Ibid.

the detection of any object, the FCW system did not provide an alert, the AEB did not activate and the Autopilot feature did not reduce the vehicle's speed.

3.3.2.1. Programming choice

This first argument is centred on the programming choice of the manufacturer. Importantly, the Autopilot feature includes an AEB feature that can respond to an object that the camera system detects in the Tesla's path but which it does not classify as a vehicle. In such instances of an unclassified object in the path of the Tesla, the AEB will only activate if the object is detected by both the camera and the radar.[82]

In a blog post just after the accident,[83] Tesla stated that the Autopilot feature did not detect the white side of the truck against the brightly lit sky – it is unclear if there were also white clouds in the sky. This amounts to an admission that it was the Tesla's camera system that did not distinguish the truck from the sky and did not detect it as an object. Hence, the AEB was not activated because the truck was not detected by the camera, recalling that for the AEB to be activated, it required detection by both the camera system and the radar.

This raises the question of correct programming choices. Was it correct, appropriate and meeting the requisite standard of care for Tesla to program the vehicle to only activate the AEB when both the camera system and the radars agree with each other in the detection of an object? The answer to this must also bear in mind that the vehicle was still in beta mode, meaning testing mode.[84]

It is a hotly debated topic whether car manufacturers should release critical safety features to be beta-tested by consumers. It appears that Tesla's Autopilot is being tested in a 'public beta' mode as it has been installed in all 70,000 of its cars since October 2014.[85] Professor Ferdinand Dudenhöffer, a prominent analyst and head of the Centre of Automotive Research at the University of Duisburg–Essen in Germany was quoted as saying that such public beta testing of vehicles was unacceptable. In an interview, he gave the opinion that '[c]ars are not toys and to launch a beta version of software with safety risks is not

---

[82] Ibid.

[83] Tesla website blog post (n 49).

[84] Olivia Solon, 'Should Tesla be "beta testing" autopilot if there is a chance someone might die?', *The Guardian* (6 July 2016) <https://www.theguardian.com/technology/2016/jul/06/tesla-autopilot-fatal-crash-public-beta-testing> accessed 23 April 2018.

[85] Ibid.

the way a company should care about the life of human beings. Just putting a sticker on it saying "customer is responsible" is a nightmare.'[86]

The public beta-testing of software has been used by technology companies over the decades to discover programming bugs quickly in products such as desktop computers and smart phones. The developer companies typically monitor and improve the software according to consumer feedback. Tesla is believed to be the first company to move public beta-testing into such a deadly arena as vehicles on public roads.

It is also perhaps due to the fact that the vehicle that Brown was in was in beta mode that he took it upon himself to test the limits of the Autopilot feature, as he turned it on and off a few times whilst ignoring the hands-on-steering-wheel warnings repeatedly. Ethical questions such as these will be considered in Chapter 6. For now, it suffices to say that, given that the car was in beta-testing mode, the more prudent way of programming to ensure the vehicle is safe for the vehicle's occupants and driver as well as other road users would be to program the activation of the AEB as an 'either/or', that is, the AEB should be activated when either the camera system or the radars detects an object – collision avoidance should be one of the top priorities of any such system and form part of the primary duties of care. It is arguable that programming the AEB to only activate when both the camera system and the radars detect an object is tantamount to a breach of the standard of care that Tesla owed to drivers of its vehicles – it could be said that Tesla was indulging in unsafe programming practices. For a vehicle in beta mode, Tesla ought to have erred on the side of caution to keep the driver and all other road users safe by programming the AEB to be activated when either the camera system or the radars detect an object.

Some may argue that programming the vehicle this way might produce too many false positives, such as stopping the vehicle for non-existent objects on the highway, which can also be dangerous. This, however, leads to the next, and second argument, that if Telsa had utilized other appropriate devices of the same or different type on the Tesla, the chances of any false positives may be reduced to zero. Tesla, however, had omitted other necessary and appropriate devices and it is in this omission that Tesla's conduct also falls below the required standard of care.

In any event, it appears that Tesla may have realized that it had made an error as it was reported that in September 2016, through wirelessly beamed software updates to its vehicles, that a new version of the Tesla software was

---

[86]   Ibid.

installed on the vehicles.[87] The new version of the software relied more on radars to identify other vehicles and potential obstacles, and to decide when to steer to avoid a problem or apply the brakes,[88] thereby removing the algorithm which simply only activated the AEB when both the camera and the radars agree with each other that there is an object ahead. The chief executive of Telsa, Elon Musk, was quoted as saying that this might have prevented the Joshua Brown crash.[89]

3.3.2.2. Choice and number of devices

This issue of the choice and number of devices on autonomous vehicles and semi-autonomous vehicles is key to the Joshua Brown crash and other Tesla crashes that will be discussed below.[90]

The Tesla Model S that Brown was in appears to have been equipped with a forward radar, a single unit of forward-looking camera, a high-precision digitally controlled electric assist braking system, a GPS system and 12 long-range ultrasonic sensors placed around the car.[91] If this suite of sensors is examined, a reasonable assessment can be made of it to determine what kind of chances Brown's Tesla Model S had in detecting the truck.

The one radar on-board enables detection of cars and other moving objects but only in a forward direction. It must be remembered that radars, whilst they do give decent range of detection, their calculation of distance is not very accurate. The facts are not clear as to whether the radar on Brown's Tesla Model S actually detected the white truck.

Tesla claimed that the long-range ultrasonic sensors are strategically placed around the Tesla Model S so that they can sense 16 feet around the car in every direction, at any speed.[92] The range of 16 feet is less than 5 metres and it is really a very short distance, especially if the vehicle is travelling at 74 miles per hour or 120 kilometres an hour. Ultrasonic sensors are typically useful for parking scenarios. Even if the ultrasonic sensors did detect the white truck, Brown's vehicle would have practically been on top of the truck when the

---

[87] Neal E Boudette, 'Tesla's self-driving system cleared in deadly crash', *The New York Times* (19 January 2017) <https://www.nytimes.com/2017/01/19/business/tesla-model-s-autopilot-fatal-crash.html> accessed 23 April 2018.

[88] Ibid.

[89] Ibid.

[90] See Sections 3.4–3.6 below.

[91] Cadie Thompson, 'Here's how Tesla's Autopilot works', *Business Insider* (1 July 2016) <http://www.businessinsider.com/how-teslas-autopilot-works-2016-7/?IR=T/#teslas-autopilot-system-is-made-up-of-multiple-sensors-placed-all-around-the-car-these-sensors-help-the-car-understand-its-environment-so-that-it-can-safely-steer-itself-in-most-highway-situations-1> accessed 23 April 2018.

[92] Ibid.

ultrasonic sensors sounded an alert; thus, any ultrasonic sensors alert would have been quite futile.

The forward-facing camera is located on the top windshield, near the rear view mirror.[93] The images captured are processed by the vehicle's computer, which attempts to interpret the images, such as detecting traffic, pedestrians, road signs and so on. How effective a computer is at detecting, categorizing and identifying an object is dependent on the AI algorithm. In the accident that killed Brown, it was proven that the algorithm is not that effective or efficient because the Tesla Model S thought the truck was not there.

There was also a GPS system on-board Brown's vehicle but GPS coordinates are used to give an estimated location of the vehicle and are generally accurate only to the last 5 metres. In any event, a GPS system cannot detect objects on its own.

There were no other devices on Brown's Tesla Model S that could have alerted Brown or the vehicle's main computer system that there was a truck ahead.

Section 3.2.7 above has expounded that, for autonomous vehicle manufacturers to meet the requisite standard of care, the vehicle must have on-board multiple redundant overlapping detection systems and these systems must be effective in their tasks. The Tesla Model S that Brown was driving did not have this in place. There are four areas of lack, which will now be addressed.

First of all, the vehicle had only one camera that was located in the upper windscreen near the rear view mirror.[94] This one camera is hardly sufficient to detect objects in both the short and long ranges, and would only have a visual field that is relatively straight-ahead. What if the one camera malfunctions or its lenses are dirty? This would result in the Tesla Model S losing its 'sight' of the road altogether. It should be noted here that in October 2016, 5 months after the accident, Tesla announced that its forthcoming vehicle, the Tesla Model 3, would have eight cameras placed all around the vehicle, providing a 360 degrees view.[95] Indeed, if Brown's Tesla Model S had had eight cameras placed all around the vehicle, it may well have detected the white truck. The truck was ahead of Brown's vehicle and towards the right of it; if there had been eight cameras on Brown's vehicle, then at least three or four cameras on the right-hand side would have detected the truck as it travelled towards the

---

[93]   Ibid.
[94]   Ibid.
[95]   Jamie Condliffe, 'Tesla announces new sensors and puts the brakes on Autopilot', *MIT Technology Review* (20 October 2016) <https://www.technologyreview.com/s/602703/tesla-announces-new-sensors-and-puts-the-brakes-on-autopilot/> accessed 23 April 2018.

intersection and turned left. This is the first breach of the requisite standard of care – insufficient cameras.

Second, the one camera was positioned at the rear view mirror of the Tesla Model S,[96] which is relatively low in height. It is questionable whether this was high enough to detect the truck given that Brown's Tesla went right underneath the truck, from one side to the other.[97] The camera may well have detected nothing in front of it as it may have been looking straight under the truck, through to the other side.

In a similar vein, the radar on Brown's vehicle was located at around the bumper bar height,[98] and this is arguably too low to have been able to detect the truck. Indeed, Tesla and the chief executive of Tesla made allusions that the radar thought that the white truck was an overhead sign that Brown's vehicle could pass under without trouble: 'the high, white side of the box truck, combined with a radar signature that would have looked very similar to an overhead sign, caused automatic braking not to fire'.[99] Tesla's chief executive tweeted on Twitter thus: 'Radar tunes out what looks like an overhead road sign to avoid false braking events'.[100] This second breach of the requisite standard of care is both inappropriately placed devices and poor algorithms that were not able to properly classify and identify real-world objects that were in fact dangerous obstacles.

Third, Musk, the chief executive of Tesla, has over the years repeatedly voiced his dislike of lidars and has flatly refused to incorporate them, even on Level 5 fully autonomous vehicles.[101] The absence of lidars on Brown's Tesla Model S is a glaring omission in the required standard of care of having multiple redundant overlapping detection systems on-board the vehicle. A lidar would have been able to detect the white truck, especially as it moved and headed towards the path of Brown's vehicle. A lidar combined with the radar on Brown's vehicle would have provided a more effective means of triggering the FCW as well as AEB than the camera plus radar combination utilized by Tesla. If there was a lidar on-board and the vehicle was programmed to activate the AEB only when both the radar and the lidar detected the object or obstacle,

---

[96]   Ibid.

[97]   NTSB (n 51), 1.

[98]   Dave Smith, 'A giant moth managed to knock out a Tesla car's Autopilot system', *Business Insider* (11 May 2016) <http://www.businessinsider.com/tesla-autopilot-knocked-out-by-moth-2016-5/?IR=T> accessed 23 April 2018.

[99]   Elon   Musk   on   Twitter   <https://twitter.com/elonmusk/status/7486259 79271045121> accessed 23 April 2018.

[100]   Andrew J Hawkins, 'Elon Musk still doesn't think LIDAR is necessary for fully driverless cars', *The Verge* (7 February 2018) <https://www.theverge.com/2018/2/7/16988628/elon-musk-lidar-self-driving-car-tesla/> accessed 23 April 2018.

[101]   Ibid.

then that may have been a satisfactory way for Tesla to discharge its duty of care, as the lidar is a highly accurate technology based on physical and material sciences, whereas the camera's detection of the truck is based on untested AI algorithms trying to categorize and identify objects. Indeed, amongst some of the circumstances revealing the unreliability of cameras in identifying objects, it has been reported that AI image-recognition software applied to data from a camera can be fooled into thinking that images of cyclists on the back of a van are genuine human cyclists.[102]

In addition, after Brown's accident, Tesla was roundly criticized for its decision to use only radar, camera and ultrasound sensors to provide data for its Autopilot feature.[103] Critics are of the opinion that lidar is an essential element in the sensor mix because, unlike a camera, it works well in low light and glare and provides more detailed and accurate data than radar or ultrasound.[104] Lidars are also more adept at detecting lane markings than the camera and radar. Furthermore, in a scorecard of the 19 companies developing self-driving vehicles, Tesla ranked last.[105] It was noted that even Tesla's own suppliers such as Nvidia have expressed doubts that the computing hardware it sells to Tesla is capable of supporting full automation reliably.[106] Hence, without the inclusion and use of lidars on its vehicles, the third breach of the requisite standard of care by Tesla is the absence of lidars, a critical piece of equipment.

Fourth, whilst Brown's Tesla Model S had a GPS on-board, there were no HD maps. HD maps are typically used as reference to compare against the dynamic three-dimensional maps created from live images fed from lidars on-board the vehicle.[107] The comparison with the reference HD maps assists the vehicle in understanding what has changed in its immediate surroundings. If there are changes, these will need to be examined carefully by the vehicle's central computer as they may well be obstacles or objects that need to be avoided. Indeed, without the HD maps, Brown's vehicle was at a handicap in detecting the white truck. Tesla's own admission was that the radar thought that the white truck was an overhead sign.[108] If Brown's Tesla had utilized HD maps, the data from them would have indicated that there are no overhead

---

[102] Jamie Condliffe (n 25).
[103] Ibid (n 25); Jamie Condliffe (n 95).
[104] Ibid.
[105] Andrew J Hawkins, 'Google nipping at Big Auto's heels in the race to build self-driving cars', *The Verge* (16 January 2018) <https://www.theverge.com/2018/1/16/16893452/detroit-auto-show-2018-google-gm-waymo-ford-tesla> accessed 23 April 2018.
[106] Ibid.
[107] See generally Chapter 2.
[108] Elon Musk (n 99).

signs at that location, and the radar and the vehicle would have been on alert for an obstacle to avoid. Hence, this fourth breach of the requisite standard of care is the non-utilization of HD maps.

3.3.3. Summary of Breach of Standard of Care on Systems

The foregoing has shown that Brown's Tesla Model S had numerous short-comings that would all amount to breaches of the standard of care Tesla owed to Brown, the owner and driver of the vehicle. The use of the hands-on-steering-wheel mechanism to ensure drivers were in fact in control of the vehicle was an ineffective system of ensuring this. Further compounding the problem was the permissible time duration of around 6 minutes where the driver need not have his hands on the steering wheel without attracting any repercussions, alerts or warnings from the vehicle. Six minutes of the driver not driving the vehicle at 74 miles per hour is clearly excessive and dangerous. The consequences of both of the above falling below the requisite standard of care was that the vehicle did not take any action even though the driver was not engaged in the driving task. As such, this resulted in the vehicle not slowing down and stopping, an action which would have prevented the crash and Brown's death.

The second major group of legally troubling acts or omissions concerns the failure to detect the white 18 wheeler truck, a massive object. The programming choice that Tesla decided upon was that the emergency braking system would only be triggered if both the camera and the radar detected an object. Whilst it is not clear whether the radar did detect the truck as it thought the truck was an overhead sign, Tesla has admitted that the camera did not detect the truck. With the camera not detecting the truck, the emergency braking system was of course not triggered, which in turn caused the collision and Brown's death. For a vehicle still in the beta-testing stage, the prudent course of action would have been to program the emergency braking system to be triggered when either the radar or the camera detected an obstacle in the path of the vehicle, even more so since there was, firstly, only one camera on the vehicle and, secondly, the system relies on AI algorithms to process the images and recognize the object. AI algorithms of this sort are largely not thoroughly tested and contain inherent errors in the way they function; hence they are not reliable on their own.

In addition to the unsafe programming choice, Brown's Tesla Model S really did not have an adequate or appropriate suite of sensors on-board. There was only one camera and only one radar on-board the Tesla Model S, both of which were located at questionable positions and height, which may have rendered them incapable of detecting the large truck. The ultrasonic sensor would have been quite useless for the task of detecting the truck as the range of the ultrasonic sensor is very short. Thus, the sensors that Tesla had fitted on

Brown's vehicle were incapable of detecting the truck. This is a breach of the standard of care required. Indeed, the industry norm is to include lidars and HD maps as part of the sensor suite and Tesla's omission in this regard falls below the requisite standard of care. While it is true that Musk has repeatedly argued that his company is being innovative in not utilizing lidars, this bare assertion cannot be sustained in light of technical information and arguments showing the dangers of not including lidars, technical information which has been substantiated through not just the crash that caused Brown's death but also in other subsequent Tesla fatal crashes.[109]

3.4.   THE STANDARD OF CARE FOR SYSTEMS – TESLA MODEL S JANUARY 2018 ACCIDENT

The accident of Brown's Tesla Model S in 2016 was not the only crash involving the Tesla Model S but it was the first one involving a fatality in the US. There have been numerous other crashes involving Tesla vehicles, indeed, Reuters tabulated a list of some 12 crashes which led to fires.[110] For many crashes, however, very little information is publicly available as to the causes. It is thus not possible to consider every Tesla vehicle that has crashed.

3.4.1.   Tesla Model S Crash Record Comparisons

According to a report by the Highway Loss Data Institute (HLDI),[111] the Tesla Model S has higher claim frequencies, which means that it crashes more frequently than other large luxury cars. The Tesla Model S is also more expensive to repair than petrol-powered large luxury cars, and it accumulates more miles on average per day than other battery-powered vehicles.[112]

The Model S was one of nine vehicles the HLDI studied in its analysis of insurance losses for all-electric vehicles. Amongst other vehicles compared were the Nissan Leaf, BMW 1 Series ActiveE, Chevrolet Spark EV, Fiat 500 Electric, Ford Focus electric, Smart ForTwo Electric Drive two-door, Smart ForTwo Electric Drive convertible and Toyota RAV4 EV. The study covered collision and property damage liability insurance policies and adjusted claim

---

[109]   This will be discussed in the following Sections 3.4–3.6.

[110]   Reuters staff, 'Factbox – Tesla faces scrutiny after Florida car accident', *Reuters* (11 May 2018) <https://www.reuters.com/article/us-tesla-crash-factbox/factbox-tesla -faces-scrutiny-after-florida-car-accident-idUSKBN1IC163> accessed 23 May 2018.

[111]   HLDI, 'Tesla Model S doesn't follow the pack on losses for electric vehicles or luxury cars', *Status Report* Vol 52 no 4 (22 June 2017) <http://www.iihs.org/ externaldata/srdata/docs/sr5204.pdf> accessed 23 April 2018.

[112]   Ibid.

frequencies for mileage. Collision insurance policies typically insure against physical damage to a vehicle in a crash if the driver is at fault. Property damage liability coverage insures against physical damage that drivers who are at fault cause to other people's vehicles and property in crashes.[113]

For those vehicles with petrol-powered versions of the same models, the HLDI compared their losses against the petrol-powered versions. Since the Tesla Model S does not have an equivalent petrol-powered version, HLDI compared the Model S against losses for conventional large luxury cars.[114]

The study found that the Teslas are driven more kilometres each day than petrol-powered luxury cars, which in real terms did not have an impact on the number of accidents claims. On average, the Tesla Model S was driven an extra 5 kilometres per day than other luxury cars, and an additional 20 kilometres a day than other electric vehicles. The study showed that, compared with the petrol-powered luxury vehicles, the Tesla's mileage-adjusted claim frequency for collision insurance policies was 37 per cent higher, the claim severity was 64 per cent higher and overall losses were 124 per cent higher. Higher claim severities refer to how expensive it is to repair collision damage relative to average estimates.[115] The HLDI study is an important objective source of information about the safety record of the Tesla Model S.

Given the numerous crashes the Tesla Model S has been involved in, it is not within the scope of this work to analyse each and every crash. Instead, the remainder of this chapter will highlight a few of the more significant crashes and examine if the causes for the crashes were due to one or more breaches of the standard of care by Tesla.

3.4.2. Tesla Model S and Stationary Objects

In January 2018, a Tesla Model S crashed into a stationary fire truck at 65 miles per hour when the Autopilot feature was driving the vehicle on a freeway in California.[116] The driver did not sustain any visible injuries.[117] On 11 May 2018, another Tesla Model S using the Autopilot feature also crashed into a stationary fire truck that was waiting at a red traffic light in South Jordan,

---

[113] Ibid, 6.

[114] Ibid, 6.

[115] Ibid, 7.

[116] Sarah Gray, 'Tesla Model S on "Autopilot" crashes into fire engine on Los Angeles freeway', *Fortune* (23 January 2018) <http://fortune.com/2018/01/23/tesla -model-s-autopilot-crashes-firetruck-los-angeles-freeway/> accessed 19 May 2018.

[117] Ibid.

Utah.[118] The Tesla Model S did not decelerate for the red traffic light and rammed into the fire truck at 60 miles per hour.[119] The driver sustained a broken ankle but the fire truck was able to be driven away, indicating that its damage was not very serious.[120] Had the vehicle not been a fire truck but a passenger vehicle, the outcome may have been deadly for those in the vehicles as the impact would have thrown the vehicles into the intersection, possibly then to be further hit by other vehicles that had the right of way.

The Tesla manual does contain a warning about stationary objects:[121]

> Traffic-Aware Cruise Control cannot detect all objects and may not brake/decelerate for stationary vehicles or objects, especially in situations when you are driving over 50 mph (80 km/h) and in situations where a vehicle you are following moves out of your driving path and a stationary vehicle or object is in front of you. Always pay attention to the road ahead and stay prepared to take immediate corrective action. Depending on Traffic-Aware Cruise Control to avoid a collision can result in serious injury or death. In addition, Traffic-Aware Cruise Control may react to vehicles or objects that either do not exist or are not in the lane of travel, causing Model S to slow down unnecessarily or inappropriately.

This appears to be a comprehensive warning and disclaimer of liability in scenarios such as the Tesla Model S crashing into a stationary fire truck. However, it is beyond the scope of this work to examine the validity of such a warning in terms of negating legal liability in light of all other statements and actions concerning the Tesla Model S by Tesla. It is however important to understand why such a warning would be in place and whether the reason for such a warning is because the standard of care has not been met in some other way.

One explanation that has been given for the crash into the stationary fire truck is the mechanisms used by Tesla. Experts suspect that the Tesla Model S system works in a way that is essentially similar to vehicles with adaptive cruise control or automated emergency braking.[122] Adaptive cruise control is a more flexible form of cruise control that slows down and speeds up the

---

[118] Peter Holley, 'Federal investigators are looking into Tesla's latest autopilot crash in Utah', *The Washington Post* (16 May 2018) <https://www.washingtonpost.com/news/innovations/wp/2018/05/16/federal-investigators-are-looking-into-teslas-latest-autopilot-crash-in-utah/?noredirect=on&utm_term=.8a5a74c55b78> accessed 19 May 2018.

[119] Ibid.

[120] Ibid.

[121] *Tesla Model S Owner's Manual* (n 73), 76.

[122] Jack Stewart, 'Why Tesla's Autopilot can't see a stopped firetruck', *Wired* (25 January 2018) <https://www.wired.com/story/tesla-autopilot-why-crash-radar/> accessed 23 April 2018.

vehicle automatically to keep pace with the vehicle in front. The driver sets the maximum speed and a radar sensor detects vehicles or traffic ahead. The radar on the vehicle would essentially 'lock' its position behind a vehicle in the lane.[123] The driver can instruct the vehicle to remain a set time, for example 3 seconds, or a set distance behind the vehicle ahead of it. It has been said that some of these adaptive cruise control systems that are radar based are designed to ignore static objects because otherwise they may have problems with false positives – and to suddenly brake on the highway for no reason can be very dangerous.[124]

Experts believe that the radar on the Tesla Model S is similar to those used in adaptive cruise control systems that are designed for detecting moving objects and seem to be not very good in detecting stationary objects.[125] The truth is that radars can detect the speed of any object but as the vehicle moves it also detects many things that it need not be concerned with, such as stationary road signs. Hence, for adaptive cruise control systems to function, the engineers make a choice and instruct the radar to ignore the stationary objects and focus on the other vehicles on the road.[126] In short, the vehicle is programmed to only focus on the objects that are moving.[127]

If indeed the radar on the Tesla Model S is like the radars used for adaptive cruise control systems, then this is a severe shortcoming that the manufacturer needs to be held accountable for. The adaptive cruise control system is quite a basic system and should not be used as one of the core means by which the vehicle drives itself.

If the Tesla Model S had on-board the requisite multiple redundant overlapping detection systems, it would have been equipped with a lidar and an HD map, both of which have different capabilities from the radar. The lidar would have been able to detect the stationary fire truck ahead without any problems, and could have triggered the brakes as a result of detecting the truck. Secondly, if the lidar was utilized in combination with an HD map, then the HD three-dimensional maps of the surroundings of the vehicle provided by the lidar, when compared with the HD map, would have been able to easily distinguish between the stationary fire truck and a road sign or some other innocuous object, and would have been able to trigger the brakes, preventing the collision.

In summary, the accidents in California in January 2018 and in Utah in May 2018, where a Tesla Model S crashed into a stationary fire truck, are yet further manifestations of Tesla's acts and omissions in not meeting the

---

[123] Ibid.
[124] Ibid.
[125] Ibid.
[126] Ibid.
[127] Ibid.

standard of care by not having the requisite multiple redundant overlapping detection systems on-board the Tesla Model S. The NTSB is investigating this accident at the time of writing, but no information has been released yet on the investigation.[128]

3.5. THE STANDARD OF CARE FOR SYSTEMS – TESLA MODEL X MARCH 2018 CRASH

The second fatality involving a Tesla vehicle in the US occurred on 23 March 2018 when a Tesla Model X SUV crashed in Mountain View, California and killed its driver, Walter Huang, while the vehicle was using the Autopilot feature.[129]

3.5.1. Tesla Model X Accident Details

Huang's Tesla Model X entered the median of a ramp on the highway and crashed into a concrete barrier about 150 yards (137 metres) into the median.[130] The crash attenuator had already been destroyed by a previous crash, hence the collision was severe as the vehicle crashed straight into the concrete barrier without any cushioning. At the time of writing, the NTSB has commenced its investigations into the crash.[131]

Tesla reported in a blog post that its data records indicated that Huang did not have his hands on the wheel in the 6 seconds before the crash.[132] According to Tesla, Huang had received several visual and one audible hands-on warnings earlier in the drive.[133] Tesla's blog post seemed to be deflecting responsibility and liability, just like its blog post on Joshua Brown's accident. Tesla stated that Huang had about 5 seconds and 150 metres of unobstructed view of the concrete divider but took no action.[134] At the time of writing, no facts have been released by the NTSB and it is unclear whether the details provided by Tesla are in fact accurate.

---

[128] David Meyer, 'Tesla is now facing 4 active U.S. government crash investigations after another fatal collision', *Fortune* (10 May 2018) <http://fortune.com/2018/05/10/tesla-ntsb-investigation-florida-crash-battery-fire/> accessed 13 May 2018.

[129] Richard Waters, 'Tesla says crash car was running on autopilot', *Financial Times* (31 March 2018) <https://www.ft.com/content/aa8fdab8-34cd-11e8-8b98-2f31af407cc8> accessed 13 May 2018.

[130] Ibid.

[131] Ibid.

[132] Tesla website blog post, 'An update on last week's accident' (30 March 2018) <https://www.tesla.com/blog/update-last-week's-accident> accessed 23 April 2018.

[133] Ibid.

[134] Ibid.

In any event, NTSB removed Tesla as a formal party to the investigation as a result of this blog post and a second public comment that Tesla made.[135] The NTSB prohibits the release of information relating to the accident itself whilst the investigation is still ongoing.[136] The NTSB guards the integrity of its investigations closely, and all participants must adhere to rules about what information they can release. The parties to investigations must sign legal agreements stating their responsibilities.[137]

To avoid the negative publicity of being thrown off the investigation, Tesla pre-emptively announced that it had withdrawn from the investigation with a covering explanation that it withdrew from the party agreement with the NTSB because the agreement required that Tesla not release information about the Autopilot feature to the public, a requirement which Tesla believed 'fundamentally' affected public safety negatively.[138] Tesla's explanation is unfortunately twisting the NTSB requirements. NTSB only prohibits the release of information about the accident; NTSB does not prohibit participants in investigations from releasing general information about their products.[139] The oft-repeated rule of thumb of NTSB is that factual information that could have been released before an accident can be released afterwards as well.[140]

It was reported that, after the initial blog post by Tesla, the NTSB did give Tesla a warning and it was only when Tesla responded to statements made by Huang's family that NTSB removed Tesla from the investigation.[141] In the response to Huang's family, who appeared on local television, Tesla made the claim that the 'only' explanation for the crash was that Huang 'was not paying attention to the road, despite the car providing multiple warnings to do so'.[142] The NTSB could not tolerate this statement as it violated NTSB's protocol for parties to an accident investigation by alleging the cause of the crash.[143]

---

[135]   Alan Levin and Ryan Beene, 'Tesla was kicked off fatal crash probe by NTSB', *Bloomberg* (12 April 2018) <https://www.bloomberg.com/news/articles/2018-04-12/tesla-withdraws-from-ntsb-crash-probe-over-autopilot-data-flap> accessed 13 May 2018.

[136]   Ibid.
[137]   Ibid.
[138]   Ibid.
[139]   Ibid.
[140]   Ibid.
[141]   Ibid.
[142]   Ibid.
[143]   Ibid.

3.5.2.   Tesla Model X Repeatedly Veered Towards the Same Barrier

When the statements of Huang's family are considered, it is understandable why Tesla felt it needed to respond with a statement as Huang's family made a direct comment that pointed to technical issues with Huang's Tesla. Huang's family had said immediately after the accident that Huang had complained of his Tesla veering towards that very same barrier on multiple occasions.[144] Huang's widow said, however, that when he tried to recreate the veering towards the barrier, it did not always occur.[145]

Huang's brother told reporters that Huang had complained that on seven to 10 occasions that the Tesla would swerve towards that same exact barrier when the Autopilot feature was enabled.[146] Huang took it to the Tesla dealership to address the issue, but the dealership was not able to duplicate the swerve towards the concrete barrier.[147] The family has provided the invoices to the investigators and these should prove to be crucial pieces of evidence. When questioned by reporters about the various occasions that Huang had sent his Tesla to the dealership to deal with the issue of it veering towards the same barrier, Tesla's response was: 'Our data shows that Tesla owners have driven this same stretch of highway with Autopilot engaged roughly 85,000 times since Autopilot was first rolled out in 2015 … There are over 200 successful Autopilot trips per day on this exact stretch of road'.[148]

The family has engaged the services of an attorney and are preparing to commence legal action against Tesla. The family's attorney summed up the perspective of the grieving family aptly when he said 'it appears that Tesla has tried to blame the victim here. It took him out of the lane that he was driving in, then it failed to brake, then it drove him into this fixed concrete barrier. We believe this would have never happened had this Autopilot never been turned on'.[149]

---

[144] Dan Noyes, 'EXCLUSIVE: Wife of man who died in Tesla crash gives emotional interview to I-Team', *ABC7 News* (10 April 2018) <http://abc7news.com/automotive/exclusive-wife-of-man-who-died-in-tesla-crash-gives-emotional-interview-to-i-team/3325177/> accessed 13 May 2018.

[145] Ibid.

[146] Dan Noyes, 'I-TEAM EXCLUSIVE: Victim who died in Tesla crash had complained about Autopilot', *ABC7 News* (28 March 2018) <http://abc7news.com/automotive/i-team-exclusive-victim-who-died-in-tesla-crash-had-complained-about-auto-pilot/3275600/> accessed 13 May 2018.

[147] Ibid.

[148] Ibid.

[149] Dan Noyes (n 144).

3.5.3. Likely Explanation of Tesla Model X Veering Problem

After Huang's crash, a number of Tesla drivers tried to recreate Huang's accident in a bid to understand why Huang's Tesla behaved the way it did. The drivers perhaps also felt that, as the technology was in beta-testing mode, they took it upon themselves, being the beta-testers, to solve the programming bug, if any. This again raises the issue of whether consumers can or should be beta-testers in technologies that can cause fatalities, such as vehicles on public roads. This will be discussed further in Chapter 6. Nevertheless, the evidence in the 2 months after the accident from other drivers is quite clear that the Autopilot feature does have problems in circumstances such as Huang's accident where the highway splits into two or where there is an off-ramp from the highway.

One of the first attempts to recreate the accident was at nighttime in Chicago, where a Tesla Model S driver was driving on the highway.[150] The lane markings just before the highway splits were not entirely clear and the video shows that the Autopilot feature locked itself on the left lane line without realizing that it was the left line marking of the soon-to-be chevron area and right-side lane marking of the upcoming ramp. It seems the Autopilot feature could not distinguish or determine where the lane markings on the left were as the right-side lane markings of the up-coming ramp were more clearly marked than the actual left line of the lane. This mistake by the Autopilot feature led the car directly into the barrier. The driver who recreated this near accident was able to brake in time but for a driver whose eyes were not on the road, there would not have been sufficient time to apply the brakes.

Around the same time the Chicago driver uploaded his video of his experiment, it was reported that the exact same scenario may have happened on 21 September 2017 in another Tesla Model S accident in Hayward, California.[151] An in-vehicle video clip from a truck, a big rig, showed the immense glare from the low morning sun as he drove towards the accident site, again where the highway splits and there is a concrete barrier divider. The Tesla driver confirmed he had the Autopilot feature on but the sun was in his eyes and by the time he wanted to take over, the car had crashed into the safety divider.[152] As

---

[150] Fred Lambert, 'Tesla owner almost crashes on video trying to recreate fatal Autopilot accident', *Electrek* (2 April 2018) <https://electrek.co/2018/04/02/tesla-fatal-autopilot-crash-recreation/> accessed 13 May 2018.

[151] Dan Noyes, 'I-TEAM EXCLUSIVE: Tesla crash in September showed similarities to fatal Mountain View accident', *ABC7 News* (4 April 2018) <http://abc7news.com/automotive/i-team-exclusive-tesla-crash-in-september-showed-similarities-to-fatal-mountain-view-accident/3302389/> accessed 13 May 2018.

[152] Ibid.

the safety divider was in its place just before the concrete divider, it functioned well and prevented the Tesla from crashing into the concrete barrier, and the driver was uninjured from the impact.

Experts interviewed by the journalist posited that the 'low sun angle could also pose a problem for the cameras that Tesla uses to drive'.[153] In both the September 2017 accident and in Huang's accident, the similarities are that both Teslas had low morning sun, both were travelling at highway speeds, both were using the Autopilot feature and both Teslas may have become confused by the road markings.[154] Like the Chicago re-enactment, the lane markings in the Hayward, California accident were also not entirely clear. The lane markings on the left of the lane on which the Tesla was travelling were faded but the lane markings just before the highway splits to the left and hence just before the chevron and barriers were solid and visibly white. Hence, it is evident that the Tesla Autopilot feature thought that the solid white line was the lane marking on the left side of the lane it was travelling on, when the solid white line was in fact the right side of the lane marking of the lane to the left of the Tesla just before the chevron area and barrier divider between the two highways.

The glare of the low morning sun was well captured in the Hayward, California accident by the camera inside the truck. The driver of the Hayward, California accident also stated that the glare of the sun blinded his vision. The cameras on the Tesla vehicles are no better than the human eye and would also have problems distinguishing lane markings on the road in the blinding sunlight. It is probably the glare from the sunlight that played a major contributing factor to the accident.

Indeed, while the Tesla dealership was not able to recreate the veering of Huang's car when he repeatedly took it in for them to check, it could well have been that the dealership was only testing Huang's vehicle at times of the day when there was no glare from the sunlight. No facts have yet been revealed of how much testing occurred and at what times of the day the Tesla dealership checked Huang's vehicle. Given that it is obvious that the Autopilot feature relies heavily on the camera inside the Tesla, it would have been reasonable and prudent for Tesla's engineers and technicians to focus on the quality of the view provided by the camera in its checking of Huang's complaints that the vehicle kept veering towards that barrier. This raises questions concerning the quality and thoroughness of Tesla in its investigation of Huang's complaints, which would also have an impact on whether Tesla did discharge its duty of care towards Huang as the owner and driver of the Tesla Model X.

---

[153] Ibid.
[154] Ibid.

Furthermore, Tesla is the only party privy to exactly how the Autopilot feature is programmed. Tesla would have full knowledge that its Autopilot feature relies on its lane-keeping feature to steer the vehicle. The lane-keeping feature in turn relies on the ability of the devices or sensors on-board the vehicle to accurately detect lane markings and to intelligently interpret them. Tesla's engineers and technicians should have been responsible and astute enough when Huang complained that his vehicle veered towards that barrier to examine the lane and road markings on that exact stretch of the road leading to the barrier. If it failed to do so, there would also be questions raised as to whether Tesla did discharge its duty of care towards Huang as the owner and driver of the Tesla Model X.

A third video clip that was uploaded to Youtube in early April 2018 showed a Tesla Model S driver driving on exactly the same stretch of road as Huang just before the accident.[155] This driver drove with the Autopilot feature turned on. As the vehicle approached the chevron area, the vehicle can be seen to veer left towards the barrier and the driver has to turn the wheel back. The video shows that the sun was shining brightly and, judging from the shadows on the ground, the vehicle was driving towards the sun with the sun most likely in front and to the left of the vehicle, hence there was plenty of glare which also made parts of the road very bright and making it difficult to discern the road markings.

From the video, it is quite clear that the vehicle started veering towards the left at the beginning or early section of the chevron area.[156] At this early section of the chevron area, the right side of the road marking was not as visibly white as the left side, which showed up clearly as a solid white line in the video. With the left side of the chevron line marking much clearer, it seemed that the Tesla thought that that was the left side of the lane it was travelling on and tagged that left chevron line as its own lane marking on the left to follow. This, of course, meant that it led the Tesla straight into the road divider and concrete barrier.

---

[155] Rob Stumpf, 'Watch Tesla Autopilot head toward location of fatal Model X accident', *The Drive* (9 April 2018) <http://www.thedrive.com/news/19931/watch-tesla-autopilot-head-toward-location-of-fatal-model-x-accident> accessed 13 May 2018.

[156] Ibid, see the video at the 38 seconds mark where there is bright sunlight making the whole road surface white and then the vehicle follows the solid white line on the left. For another video which clearly shows the Tesla Model S not able to accurately detect the lane markings to drive within, see Ryan Felton, 'Don't use Tesla's autopilot like this', *Jalopnik* (2 March 2017) <https://jalopnik.com/dont-use-teslas-autopilot-like-this-1792896205> accessed 13 May 2018.

3.5.4.   Breaches of Standard of Care – Tesla Model X March 2018 Crash

From the various videos that have been uploaded onto the Internet, a few conclusions can be drawn with regards to Tesla's acts or omissions concerning Huang's Tesla. While it is true that the Tesla vehicle is a Level 2 automation vehicle, the contextual background also needs to be taken into consideration. First, Tesla has repeatedly expounded the convenience virtues of its Autopilot feature, which leads drivers and consumers to believe that the Autopilot feature is capable of much more than Level 2 automation. Second, the name of the feature itself being named Autopilot misleads consumers and drivers into thinking that the vehicle is capable of driving itself.

Third, it has been countered by Tesla that Huang did not have his hands on the steering wheel in the final 6 seconds; even if this is true, it still harks back to Tesla's own failing in allowing drivers to not have their hands on the steering wheel but still permitting the vehicle to continue moving. This has already been discussed above.[157] Furthermore, there is also the argument that, given Tesla's own messages about the inflated capabilities of its Autopilot feature mixed in with what seems like hollow reminders that drivers should keep their hands on the steering wheel coupled with a system that allows drivers to go hands-free for at least 6 minutes, drivers and consumers have been misled into believing or wanting to believe that their Teslas are capable of self-driving.

Fourth, Huang had complained that his Tesla kept veering towards that very same barrier and had taken his vehicle on numerous occasions to the Tesla dealership for inspection. There is room to argue that the Tesla inspections were not thorough and quite likely negligent. In around 2 weeks after Huang's accident, other Tesla drivers were able to take their Teslas on test drives to determine reasons why the Tesla might have veered left towards the barrier and in around 2 weeks, these drivers provided sufficient evidence as to the reason. Yet Tesla was not able to provide Huang with any assistance or explanations after he brought his vehicle to them for testing on numerous occasions. This is despite the fact that Tesla has proprietary knowledge of how its own vehicles are programmed and put together whereas the ordinary Tesla drivers do not have this technical knowledge and advantage. Tesla's failure in this regard would point towards inspections and testing of Huang's vehicle that fell well below what a reasonable person in Tesla's position would have done, thereby falling below the required standard of care.

Fifth, the Autopilot feature is still at the beta-testing stage, which means that consumers are the testers of the vehicle's technologies. As such, it is arguable

---

[157] See Section 3.3.1.

that Tesla has a higher duty of care towards Tesla owners and drivers. This means that, when Huang brought his Tesla Model X into the dealership repeatedly for inspection, Tesla had a higher threshold of care to meet and it should have done much more in its testing and investigations. Indeed, as the standard of care for beta-testing vehicles should be higher, requiring Tesla to do more to meet its duty of care, Tesla evidently failed to meet this standard of care when it either did not identify or was not capable of identifying the issues and problems that Huang raised. Yet ordinary drivers were able to recreate the very same veering complaints that worried Huang. Tesla's breach of the standard of care may even fall within the res ipsa loquitor doctrine.

Sixth, the Autopilot feature took the vehicle out of a lane and entered the chevron area of a ramp on the highway as if it was a lane and crashed into a concrete barrier that it did not detect. The camera and radar on Huang's Tesla Model X obviously were defective as they did not or could not recognize the concrete barrier. In addition, the Tesla Model X did not have on-board multiple redundant overlapping detection systems, which would have detected the concrete barrier and instructed the brakes to be applied. In essence, even though there was a wrongful act of taking the vehicle out of its lane and straight towards the concrete barrier, there was no secondary or additional system to detect the concrete barrier and to prevent the crash from occurring. If the Tesla Model X had had a lidar on-board, it would have been able to detect the concrete barrier as an obstacle and ordered the brakes to be applied. Alternatively, if the vehicle had utilized HD maps, these would have been able to inform the Autopilot feature that it was heading straight towards a concrete barrier.

Tesla's omission to utilize multiple redundant overlapping detection systems appears to be a substantial cause of the accident, since if there had been lidars and HD maps utilized by the Tesla Model X, the crash would not have occurred. This is again a clear breach of the standard of care that Tesla owed to Huang as a Tesla owner and driver.

Seventh, Huang's Tesla accident can in some ways be considered an incident that is a level more severe than the January 2018 Tesla Model S crash into a stationary fire truck. Huang's crash also involved the Tesla crashing into a stationary object, the concrete barrier, which the Tesla's radar sensor did not detect or was programmed to ignore.[158] In Huang's accident, however, his Tesla Model X took an earlier step of taking the vehicle out of its lane and then, secondly, crashing into a stationary object. In this sense, the vehicle was malfunctioning in a cumulative two-step process. The act of taking the Tesla out of its lane was the result of both a wrongful act and a wrongful omission by Tesla.

---

[158] See Section 3.4.2.

It was a wrongful act because the Tesla Model X was not able to correctly identify where the lane was located and mistook the chevron marking to be the lane it was travelling on and proceeded to follow that chevron marking, leading the Tesla straight into the concrete barrier. Without examining the Tesla Model X software and hardware, it is not possible to determine whether this was due to an inherent limitation in using a camera-based system, or whether this was due to poor AI image recognition software utilized by Tesla, that is, a programming bug. In any event, it is not critical as the videos from other Tesla drivers have shown how the Tesla vehicle has been programmed to behave; these alone are sufficient evidence that there was a failure to meet the required standard of care in keeping the Tesla within its own lane.

There was also a wrongful omission by Tesla because it failed to utilize multiple redundant overlapping detection systems which would have better enabled the Tesla to stay within its lane and not drive into the chevron area. Had the Tesla been equipped with lidars and HD maps, it would have been more adept at recognizing lane markings and more accurately locating where its lane was in order to stay within its lane, instead of wandering into the chevron area.

To be clear, from the foregoing, the missing multiple redundant overlapping detection systems caused not just the non-detection of the concrete barrier ahead of Huang's vehicle, but also the Autopilot feature to take the Tesla Model X out of its lane into the chevron area and straight into the concrete barrier.

This combination of two missteps in the two-step process by the Tesla Model X constitutes not one, but two breaches of the standard of care by Tesla towards Huang, the owner and driver of Tesla's vehicle.

Lastly, it should be noted for completeness that, even if Huang did not have his hands on the steering wheel for the final 6 seconds, this does not negate any duty of care owed by Tesla to Huang, nor would it negate any breaches of the standard of care. At best, it would mean that Huang was contributorily negligent.

3.6.   THE STANDARD OF CARE – TESLA MODEL S CRASH IN CHINA

It is currently believed that the first Tesla vehicle crash involving a fatality occurred in China on 20 January 2016.[159] Tesla managed to keep the China

---

[159] Christian Shepherd, 'Tesla sued in China over fatal crash', *Financial Times* (20 September 2016) <https://www.ft.com/content/80c45ad6-7ef0-11e6-bc52-0c 7211ef3198> accessed 13 May 2018.

fatality away from the public eye initially but it was exposed in September 2016 when the deceased driver's father and owner of the crashed Tesla Model S, Gao Jubin, commenced legal proceedings against Tesla China and a local dealership in Chaoyang District People's Court of Beijing for his son's death in the accident where the Tesla's Autopilot feature was driving the vehicle.[160]

The Tesla Model S slammed into a road sweeper on a highway near Handan in the province of Hebei, south of Beijing, which caused the driver Gao Yaning to die instantly.[161] A video from the in-vehicle dash camera showed the horrific crash.[162] It is unclear if the road sweeper was stationary or moving slowly, as most road sweepers move when they are cleaning the roads. The footage showed that the Tesla was travelling at a constant speed until it crashed into the road sweeper. Even just before the collision, the Tesla Model S did not decelerate.[163]

3.6.1. Denials of the Engagement of the Autopilot Feature

Initially, Tesla said that it had not been able to determine whether the Autopilot feature was being utilized when the Handan accident occurred.[164] Just after the September 2016 hearing, Tesla stated that there was 'no evidence that Autopilot was engaged at the time of the accident', adding that, regardless, the Autopilot feature was not the 'cause' of the accident, owing to the technology only being a 'driver assistance system that supplements an attentive driver'.[165]

Indeed, at the time of the hearing, Tesla had said that it could not confirm whether the Autopilot feature was engaged due to damage to the vehicle, rendering it 'physically incapable of transmitting log data to our servers'.[166] Tesla even stated that it had 'tried repeatedly to work with Mr Gao to investigate the cause of the crash, but Mr Gao has not provided us with any additional information that would allow us to do so'.[167]

These quite astounding claims made by Tesla were rebutted in court by Gao's lawyer. The plaintiff's counsel pointed out that the consistent speed of travel for 8 minutes before the collision, and the failure to change lanes or

---

[160] Ibid.
[161] Ibid.
[162] Guy Birchall, 'Death by robocars', *The Sun* (15 September 2016) <https://www.thesun.co.uk/news/1787336/shocking-dashcam-footage-shows-horror-tesla-crash-that-killed-driver-while-car-was-on-autopilot/> accessed 13 May 2018.
[163] Christian Shepherd (n 159).
[164] Guy Birchall (n 162).
[165] Christian Shepherd (n 159).
[166] Ibid (n 159).
[167] Ibid (n 159).

swerve suggest that the Autopilot feature was active.[168] Furthermore, a Tesla customer service staff had called Gao shortly after the collision informing him that his Tesla's airbags had exploded,[169] hence the Tesla must have been transmitting data up until the crash,[170] which would mean that Tesla's initial claim that the vehicle was so damaged that it was physically incapable of transmitting log data could not stand.

Finally, more than 2 years after the accident, in February 2018, Tesla admitted that, when Gao Yaning's vehicle crashed into the road sweeper truck, the Autopilot feature was engaged.[171]

3.6.2. Non-disclosure of Crashes Involving Autopilot Feature

It is difficult to believe that it would have taken Tesla 2 years to ascertain whether the Autopilot feature was driving the car at the time of the accident in China. In addition, this raises questions concerning Tesla's lack of transparency in bringing crashes that occur as a result of the Autopilot feature being engaged to the attention of the public. This is critically important as the technology on the Tesla is still at the public beta-testing stage. As such, Tesla has a duty of care to inform the users of its technology if and when crashes occur, largely so that users can take precautions and be fully informed – that is why the technology is labelled as at the beta-testing stage.

Although the fatal crash in China occurred in January 2016, Tesla did not release a statement until a report from China's official state broadcaster CCTV in September 2016, which reported on the court case.[172] This undue delay in informing the public of a fatal crash for a technology still at the public beta-testing stage points to not just reckless indifference to human life but also a failure to meet the required standard of care owed to Tesla drivers and owners to provide timely notification of fatal accidents involving its Autopilot feature.

---

[168] Ibid (n 159).

[169] Ryan Felton, 'Two years on, a father is still fighting Tesla over Autopilot and his son's fatal crash', *Jalopnik* (27 February 2018) <https://jalopnik.com/two-years-on-a-father-is-still-fighting-tesla-over-aut-1823189786> accessed 13 May 2018.

[170] Christian Shepherd (n 159).

[171] ECNS, 'Tesla confirms "Autopilot" engaged in fatal crash in China' (28 February 2018) <http://www.ecns.cn/2018/02-28/293992.shtml> accessed 13 May 2018.

[172] Jay Ramey, 'Latest Tesla lawsuit: Family of China crash victim sues EV maker', *AutoWeek* (20 September 2016) <http://autoweek.com/article/technology/family-man-killed-tesla-crash-china-sues-automaker> accessed 13 May 2018.

3.6.3. Breaches of the Standard of Care for Systems

The facts are unclear as to how the collision occurred and what caused it. If the road sweeper truck was indeed stationary, then all of the arguments presented above in relation to Teslas crashing into stationary objects would be applicable here.[173] Such a scenario would implicate poor use of sensors such as the camera and radar, which cannot detect or have been programmed to not detect stationary objects. Also implicated would be the failure of Tesla in its omission of equipping the Tesla with multiple redundant overlapping detection systems, such as lidars and HD maps, which would have been able to detect stationary objects with high accuracy.

If the road sweeper truck was moving slowly as it cleaned the road, then it could be equipment malfunction on the Tesla Model S or some other reason related to the inability of the camera and radar to correctly identify or recognize the road sweeper truck, whether it be hardware or software inability. Or it could be that the road sweeper truck was moving so slowly that the camera and radar mistook it for a stationary object. This could be highly likely as the radar is often only accurate to several feet.[174] If this was the case, it then raises the issue of Tesla falling below the required standard of care by not utilizing redundant overlapping detection systems and not equipping the Tesla with lidars and HD maps which would have been able to detect the road sweeper truck and take appropriate actions such as applying the brakes.

One thing that is obvious from the video clip from the dash camera is that the road sweeper truck was at the extreme left edge of the road as if it was sweeping the road and it was not entirely inside the marked lane.[175] As such, it would suggest that the Tesla's camera and radar were not able to detect it as it was not directly in front of the Tesla Model S within the lane markings, something which has been discussed above.[176] This again suggests that Tesla breached the required standard of care in its omission of utilizing redundant overlapping detection systems, for had the Tesla Model S been equipped with lidars and HD maps, then it would have been able to detect the road sweeper truck and take appropriate actions.

From the dash camera video clip which also recorded the sounds inside the vehicle,[177] just before the Tesla Model S crashed into the road sweeper truck, there was no warning alert of any sort. Apart from the shortcomings of the

---

[173] See Section 3.4.2 above.

[174] See Chapter 2 and Harry Surden and Mary-Anne Williams, 'Techonological opacity, predictability, and self-driving cars' (2016) 38 Cardozo Law Review 121, 145.

[175] Guy Birchall (n 162).

[176] See Section 3.3.2 above.

[177] Ryan Felton (n 169).

Autopilot feature which did not detect the road sweeper truck, the automatic emergency braking system (which functions independently of the Autopilot feature) on the Tesla Model S should have alerted the driver of a potential hazard ahead. The AEB system should automatically apply the brakes if the driver does not react in time. In the case of Gao's accident, the emergency braking system did not sound an alert, let alone apply the brakes. This would suggest that the emergency braking system was not triggered. This situation may be akin to Joshua Brown's accident already discussed above, that is, perhaps the emergency braking system was not triggered because the camera system and the radar system did not both detect an object ahead.[178] Recall that Tesla had programmed its vehicles such that the emergency braking system would only be triggered if both the camera and radar systems agreed with each other that there was an obstacle ahead.[179] This way of programming the emergency braking system, as already discussed above, would amount to falling below the standard of care required of technology that is still at the beta-testing stage.

3.6.4.   Negligent Misstatements and Misrepresentations

The accident in China also highlights a critically important issue when things go amiss with technology – it is not easy for the claimant to extract technical information from the defendant. At the court hearing in Beijing in 2016, Gao requested an independent investigation of the cause of the crash. Gao insisted that the investigation should be conducted by a third party, and not Tesla.[180] As at February 2018, the investigation and legal suit appears to be still ongoing and there have been no further reports as at early May 2018.[181]

Given the lack of information about the workings of the Tesla Model S and why the crashed happened, Gao sued Tesla China and the dealership that sold the car for misleading buyers.[182] Gao and his family claimed that the salespeople had exaggerated the Autopilot feature's capabilities. They also sought a public apology for false advertising as well as 10,000 yuan (around US$1500) as compensation for the grief they have suffered because of their

---

[178]   See sections 3.3.2–3.3.3.
[179]   Ibid.
[180]   Rose Yu, 'Family of Driver Killed in Tesla Crash in China Seeks Court Investigation', *The Wall Street Journal* (20 September 2016) <https://www.wsj.com/articles/family-of-driver-killed-in-tesla-crash-in-china-seeks-court-investigation-1474351855> accessed 13 May 2018.
[181]   Ryan Felton (n 169).
[182]   Rose Yu (n 180).

son's death.[183] Additionally, Gao requested that the dealership cease using the Chinese equivalent of the word 'Autopilot' when promoting Tesla vehicles.[184]

The compensation amount sought has since been amended to 5 million yuan (around US$750,000) and if Gao is successful in his legal action, he has plans to use some of the money to start a charity fund 'to warn more Tesla owners not to use Autopilot'.[185]

Gao told journalists that he had had a conversation with his son, Yaning, after purchasing the Tesla Model S, where Yaning had explained to his father that a Tesla salesperson told him that the Autopilot feature can handle all driving functions and the driver could just sleep on the highway and leave the Tesla vehicle alone; the vehicle will know when to brake or turn, and the driver can listen to music or drink coffee.[186]

The issue of misleading the public about the capabilities of Tesla's beta-testing stage technology came into public discussion in China in August 2016 just before the court hearing of Gao's legal claim when a Tesla owner, Luo Zhen, posted online a dash camera video clip of his Tesla Model S sideswiping a parked car on a Beijing highway.[187] Luo stated that his vehicle was using the Autopilot feature and his car hit a vehicle parked half off the road, destroying the parked vehicle's side mirror and scraping both cars, but causing no injuries.[188] Luo admitted he was looking at his phone or the in-vehicle navigation at the time of the accident, only looking up every few seconds. However, Luo also claimed that he had been misled about the vehicle's capabilities.[189]

Luo was adamant that there was a fault in the Autopilot feature and stressed that Tesla's sales staff strongly promoted the system as 'self-driving'.[190] He told *Reuters* reporters that the 'impression they give everyone is that this is self-driving, this isn't assisted driving'.[191] Luo contended that Tesla uses the immature technology as a sales and promotion tactic but Tesla does not take responsibility for the safety of the functions, which was what led him to upload his dash camera video clip and criticisms of the company.[192]

---

[183] Ibid (n 180).
[184] Ibid (n 180).
[185] Ryan Felton (n 169).
[186] Ibid (n 169).
[187] Jake Spring, '"Self-driving" in spotlight again as China sees first Tesla autopilot crash', *Reuters* (10 August 2016) <https://www.reuters.com/article/us-tesla-china-crash-idUSKCN10L0P4> accessed 13 May 2018.
[188] Ibid.
[189] Ibid.
[190] Ibid.
[191] Ibid.
[192] Ibid.

Reuters conducted interviews with four other unconnected Tesla drivers in Beijing, Shanghai and Guangzhou, who all also indicated that the message conveyed by front-line sales staff was not the same as Tesla's more clear-cut statements that the system is not 'self-driving' but an advanced driver assistance system.[193]

The Tesla owners interviewed by Reuters all confirmed that Tesla salespeople described the vehicle's function in Chinese as 'self-driving' and even removed their hands from the steering wheel while demonstrating the vehicle.[194] One Shanghai resident, Mao Mao, told Reuters that they 'all described it as being able to drive itself'.[195]

The term 'self-driving' is one that Tesla avoids using in English. However, the term 'zi dong jia shi' appeared several times on Tesla's Chinese website, which is literally translated to mean 'self-driving'.[196] It is also the same term used for an airplane autopilot, which is also why consumers such as Gao and Luo would have been misled into believing that the Tesla Model S is self-driving, that is, a Level 5 automation vehicle.[197]

When questioned by Reuters, Tesla's response was a plain denial: 'We have never described autopilot as an autonomous technology or a "self-driving car," and any third-party descriptions to this effect are not accurate'.[198]

After Luo's post and video clip generated a substantial amount of online discussion in China, in mid-August 2016, Tesla toned down its description of the Autopilot feature on its Chinese website and in other advertising materials from 'zi dong jia shi' to 'zi dong fu zhu jia shi', which translates to autonomous/automatic assisted driving and thus alludes to more of an assisted role in driving.[199] At the same time, Tesla's China-based sales staff was also instructed to make the Autopilot system's limitations clear[200] and Tesla also retrained staff in China on the proper demonstration protocols for the Autopilot feature.[201]

It would seem that Tesla's choice of Chinese words used for its Autopilot feature and the behaviour of Tesla's dealerships in China did confuse the consumers into believing that their Tesla vehicles were self-driving vehicles. As such, the misleading statements and misrepresentations concerning the

---

[193] Ibid.
[194] Ibid.
[195] Ibid.
[196] Ibid.
[197] Ibid.
[198] Ibid.
[199] Rose Yu (n 180).
[200] Ibid (n 180).
[201] Jay Ramey (n 172).

technology on Tesla vehicles suggest a failure to meet the requisite standard of care owed by Tesla to Tesla vehicle owners and drivers. It would also appear that this was what happened to Gao's son when he was misled about the nature of the Tesla Model S and its capabilities, and acted upon the factually incorrect beliefs, resulting in his death.

3.7.   THE STANDARD OF CARE – UBER PEDESTRIAN ACCIDENT 2018

On 18 March 2018, 49-year-old Elaine Herzberg became the first pedestrian in the US to be struck and killed by an autonomous vehicle.[202] The accident occurred in Tempe, Arizona when Herzberg was pushing her bicycle across the road at nighttime.[203] Uber was test driving the autonomous vehicle, a Volvo sport utility vehicle (SUV), in autonomous mode at the time of the crash with a safety driver behind the wheel.[204] Herzberg was taken to hospital, where she later died from her injuries. Uber's female safety driver was the only person inside the autonomous vehicle at the time of the crash, and she did not sustain any injuries.[205]

Uber began testing its autonomous vehicles in Arizona in February 2017 after it had refused to apply for a $150 permit to test its vehicles in San Francisco, as required by California's Department of Motor Vehicles.[206] After the Arizona accident, Uber took the ethical step of ceasing the testing of its autonomous vehicles from public roads in Arizona as well as in the cities of San Francisco, Toronto and Pittsburgh.[207] The NTSB is investigating the accident with Uber as a participant and the investigations are ongoing at the time of writing.[208]

Like many autonomous vehicles that are being trialled, the Uber autonomous vehicle was equipped with many cameras and sensors that will provide crucial evidence for determining the cause of the crash. However, what shocked many people familiar with autonomous vehicle technology was when the Tempe Police Department released a video of the accident showing both

---

[202] Andrew J Hawkins, 'Uber halts self-driving tests after pedestrian killed in Arizona', *The Verge* (19 March 2018) <https://www.theverge.com/2018/3/19/17139518/uber-self-driving-car-fatal-crash-tempe-arizona> accessed 13 May 2018.

[203] Ibid.

[204] Ibid.

[205] Ibid.

[206] Ibid.

[207] Ibid.

[208] Ibid.

the interior and exterior views.[209] The exterior view was from a dash camera that showed Herzberg emerging from seeming darkness from the left side of the road. The interior view was that of Uber's safety driver, a woman hired to watch and to take control of the autonomous vehicle if the technology failed. She was unfortunately looking down, probably at her lap, immediately prior to the accident, instead of paying attention to the road. Largely because its safety driver was not paying attention to the road, Uber sought and reached a settlement with Herzberg's husband and daughter.[210]

Whilst the road may have appeared dark in the video clip, it may not have been as dark as the video suggested as the night was clear and streetlights were lit. Herzberg was visible in front of the vehicle for nearly 2 seconds before the collision. It was a wide-open road and she had nearly crossed the entire four-lane, empty road before being struck by the front right side of the vehicle.

Many autonomous vehicle developers were puzzled as to why the accident had occurred as the Uber autonomous vehicle appeared to have sufficient sensors and other devices on-board that should have been able to detect Herzberg.[211] In the days after the accident, many were searching for reasons why the Uber autonomous vehicle did not stop for the crossing pedestrian. Was it because the autonomous vehicle did not detect Herzberg? If so, why did it not detect her? Or was it because the autonomous vehicle did detect Herzberg but was programmed to disregard or ignore her? Or worse still, was the AI algorithm so poorly designed that the developers had no idea how it would function in the circumstances of that night?

The NTSB is still investigating the accident but on 24 May 2018 it released a Preliminary Report, which shed some light on what might have happened. Until the NTSB concludes its investigations and reveals the reasons behind the crash, with the information from the Preliminary Report, it is worthwhile examining some of the possible reasons.

---

[209] Sam Levin, 'Uber crash shows "catastrophic failure" of self-driving technology, experts say', *The Guardian* (22 March 2018) <https://www.theguardian.com/technology/2018/mar/22/self-driving-car-uber-death-woman-failure-fatal-crash-arizona> accessed 13 May 2018.

[210] Ellen Tannam, 'Software bug reportedly behind fatal self-driving Uber accident', *Siliconrepublic* (8 May 2018) <https://www.siliconrepublic.com/companies/uber-bug-crash> accessed 13 May 2018.

[211] Aarian Marshall, 'The Uber Crash won't be the last shocking self-driving death', *Wired* (31 March 2018) <https://www.wired.com/story/uber-self-driving-crash-explanation-lidar-sensors/> accessed 13 May 2018.

3.7.1. NTSB's Preliminary Report

The NTSB's Preliminary Report stated that Uber's autonomous vehicle was factory equipped with several advanced driver assistance functions by Volvo Cars, the original manufacturer, including a collision avoidance function with AEB, as well as functions for detecting driver alertness and road sign information.[212] All of these Volvo functions are disabled by Uber when the test autonomous vehicle was being tested in the computer control mode such as during test drives but are operational when the vehicle is operated in manual control mode.[213] The justification provided by Uber for this was that the 'developmental self-driving system relies on an attentive operator to intervene if the system fails to perform appropriately during testing'.[214] This is probably the reason why Uber sought a settlement with Herzberg's family as Uber's operator was not attentive at the time of the accident.

3.7.2. Disabling of Emergency Braking System

According to the Preliminary Report, the data from Uber's autonomous vehicle showed that the radar and lidar detected Herzberg about 6 seconds before impact, when the vehicle was travelling at 43 miles per hour.[215] At 1.3 seconds before the collision, the autonomous vehicle determined that the emergency braking system needed to be triggered but Uber had disabled the emergency braking system during test drives, to purportedly reduce 'the potential for erratic vehicle behaviour'.[216] Instead it relied on its safety driver to intervene in such emergencies.[217]

It is unclear what exactly Uber meant by 'the potential for erratic vehicle behaviour' but it would appear to suggest that Uber's autonomous vehicles would suddenly apply the emergency brakes for objects that the autonomous vehicle did not need to avoid, such as a flying paper bag. This tends to indicate that Uber's sensors and detection technologies were not mature and that its

---

[212] NTSB, *Preliminary Report Highway HWY18MH010* <https://www.ntsb.gov/investigations/AccidentReports/Reports/HWY18MH010-prelim.pdf>, accessed 30 May 2018, 2.

[213] Ibid.

[214] Ibid.

[215] Ibid.

[216] Ibid.

[217] Ibid.

autonomous vehicles had previously had problems with false positives.[218] This is something that will be further discussed in Chapter 4.[219]

Of importance for the current discussion is that Uber's autonomous vehicle was not designed to alert the operator that emergency brakes needed to be applied.[220] Uber did not have a warning system to alert the safety driver who would take control in an emergency. This, in itself, would appear to be a design fault of the overall system, and also falls short of the standard of care required. A reasonable person would have, after disabling the emergency braking system, at the very least, designed the autonomous vehicle such that it would alert the safety driver, probably through loud sounds, that the brakes needed to be applied urgently. From the Preliminary Report, Herzberg was about 25 metres ahead of the autonomous vehicle at 1.3 seconds before collision.[221] A warning system sounded at that time could have saved Herzberg's life as the safety driver could have braked and swerved.

Furthermore, on an autonomous vehicle that has had the emergency braking system disabled, a reasonable person would probably have installed a routine warning system, perhaps through sounds, that it has detected a potential obstacle ahead. This would give the safety driver, however inattentive, time to pay attention and react. In the case of Herzberg, Uber's autonomous vehicle detected her 6 seconds before the collision. If Uber's vehicle had had this warning system installed, then the safety driver would have had ample time to look up, brake or swerve as necessary. So again, the failure by Uber to implement such a warning system on its autonomous vehicles points to a failure to take due care.

3.7.3.   Only One Lidar on Uber's SUV

After the accident, journalists discovered that, when Uber switched its autonomous vehicles from Ford Fusion vehicles to Volvo SUVs, it reduced the number of lidars on its autonomous vehicles.[222] This meant that its autonomous

---

[218]   Tim Bradshaw and Shannon Bond, 'Self-driving car crash report highlights Uber safety shortcomings', *Financial Times* (25 May 2018) <https://www.ft.com/content/2c3d8efc-5fb2-11e8-9334-2218e7146b04> accessed 30 May 2018, 2.

[219]   See Chapter 4, Section 4.3.4.2.

[220]   NTSB, *Preliminary Report Highway HWY18MH010* (n 212).

[221]   Ibid, 3.

[222]   Heather Somerville, Paul Lienert and Alexandria Sage, 'Uber's use of fewer safety sensors prompts questions after Arizona crash', *Reuters* (28 March 2018) <https://www.reuters.com/article/us-uber-selfdriving-sensors-insight/ubers-use-of-fewer-safety-sensors-prompts-questions-after-arizona-crash-idUSKBN1H337Q> accessed 13 May 2018.

vehicle had more blind spots than its own earlier generation of autonomous vehicles, as well as those of its competitors.[223]

It was revealed that Uber's Ford Fusion vehicles had seven lidars, seven radars and 20 cameras. Uber's Volvo SUVs were equipped with one lidar, 10 radars and seven cameras.[224] The huge reduction in lidars may or may not have played a role in this particular accident but having only one roof-mounted lidar sensor compared with seven lidar units on the older Ford Fusion models certainly raises many questions about blind spots given that, of the three types of sensors, lidars are the best at detecting human flesh and lidars provide the greatest accuracy.[225]

Uber's competitors Waymo, Alphabet Inc.'s autonomous vehicles unit, utilizes six lidar sensors on its autonomous vehicles, while General Motors Co.'s autonomous vehicles have five.[226] These typically comprise a central rooftop lidar with multiple, smaller units around the car to augment the central rooftop one. This arrangement provides more complete coverage of the road.[227]

Some experts believed that, by utilizing only a single lidar, Uber introduced a blind zone around the perimeter of the SUV that cannot fully detect pedestrians.[228] The lidar on the Uber autonomous vehicle was manufactured by Velodyne. It detects objects in a 360 degree circle around the car, but has a narrow vertical range that prevents it from detecting obstacles low to the ground.[229] When asked by reporters about the blind spot, Uber referred questions on the blind spot to Velodyne, which acknowledged that, with only one rooftop lidar, there is an approximately 3 metre blind spot around a vehicle.[230] Velodyne also confirmed that more sensors are necessary in order to avoid pedestrians; in particular, side lidars are necessary to enable pedestrians to be seen and avoided, especially at night.[231]

In an Uber diagram of the Ford Fusion autonomous vehicle, it noted that the 'front, rear and wing-mounted lidar modules aid in the detection of obstacles in close proximity to the vehicle, as well as smaller ones that can get lost in blind spots'.[232] In an attempt to justify the massive reduction in the number of lidars, Uber stated that it chose to rely more on radars to detect obstacles that may

---

[223] Ibid.
[224] Ibid.
[225] See Chapter 2.
[226] Heather Somerville, Paul Lienert and Alexandria Sage (n 222).
[227] Ibid.
[228] Ibid.
[229] Ibid.
[230] Ibid.
[231] Ibid.
[232] Ibid.

end up being in those blind spots.[233] Whether the radar is a reliable sensor for such a task is questionable as the radar is not as reliable as the lidar in detecting creatures such as humans.

There is a further issue of Uber moving from a sedan, namely, the Ford Fusion, to a much taller vehicle, the Volvo SUV. This means that the single lidar is now located higher up on top of the vehicle, further reducing its ability to see low-lying objects such as a person's legs or the wheels of a bicycle.[234]

From the technical specifications expounded thus far, it would appear that having one single lidar on top of the rooftop of an autonomous vehicle would not be how a reasonable person would design an autonomous vehicle given that there will be a blind spot zone around it that may not be compensated for by the use of other kinds of sensors such as the radar. As such, it seems to show a lack of due care by Uber in the way it has implemented the devices on its autonomous vehicles.

This breach of the required standard of care, however, may or may not explain Herzberg's accident because she was not in the blind zone of Uber's autonomous vehicle. She was well in front of the autonomous vehicle initially and not within the 3 metre blind spot around the autonomous vehicle. The analysis does not end here however.

According to the Preliminary Report, Uber's autonomous vehicle had 'classified the pedestrian as an unknown object, as a vehicle, and then as a bicycle with varying expectations of future travel path'.[235] Herzberg was pushing a bicycle, which presumably was made of metal, and as such, the 10 radars should have been able to detect her bicycle without any trouble. Yet the 10 radars took some time to classify the bicycle as a bicycle – this would point to issues with the competency of Uber's software in being able to classify objects correctly.

Furthermore, it would appear that Uber's autonomous vehicle never properly classified Herzberg as a human being, a pedestrian. The radars detected the metal on the bicycle but the radars and lidar were not able to detect or classify Herzberg – it is as if Herzberg did not exist as far as the autonomous vehicle was concerned. As discussed in Chapter 2, this is not entirely surprising given the limitations of radars: radars work best at detecting metals, not human beings.[236] There was only one lidar on the autonomous vehicle; lidars are effective at detecting humans. Could the one lidar have malfunctioned that night? Or was it defective in some other way? Apart from the problem of

---

[233] Ibid.
[234] Ibid.
[235] NTSB, *Preliminary Report Highway HWY18MH010* (n 212).
[236] See Chapter 2, Section 2.2.3.

creating a blind zone around the perimeter of the vehicle, by installing only one lidar in the sensor suite, Uber was also in breach of the standard of care because it is well known that machines (especially fragile constantly spinning machinery) do break down or malfunction, which is why there is a need for multiple redundant overlapping detection systems on autonomous vehicles. By having a single lidar, there was no extra redundant system for the autonomous vehicle to unequivocally detect human beings.

As both Herzberg and her bicycle were moving perpendicular to the vehicle, this would have given the lidar and radars a larger cross-section to reflect their signals, thus it remains to be seen exactly why Uber's autonomous vehicle never detected and classified Herzberg as a human being, but a bicycle.

From the foregoing, it would appear that, in the case of Herzberg's accident, there was an inadequate number of lidars on Uber's autonomous vehicle. This failure may have been the cause of the autonomous vehicle failing to stop for Herzberg.

3.7.4. Software and Algorithms on Uber's SUV?

Other possibilities for Uber's SUV failing to stop for Herzberg include software failures or poor software design, such as poor algorithm design.

Indeed, around 2 months after the accident, there were leaks to the media suggesting that the fatal crash was caused by Uber's autonomous vehicle software.[237] Uber was unable to comment on the leaks as the investigation by NTSB was ongoing.[238]

Anonymous sources had told reporters that the autonomous vehicle's sensors did detect Herzberg as she crossed the street, but Uber's software decided that an immediate reaction to Herzberg and her bicycle was unnecessary.[239] It seemed that Uber's software had made the decision that Herzberg and her bicycle was a 'false positive', and made the further decision that the SUV did not need to stop.[240]

This issue of false positives and false negatives is one of the fundamental challenges in the development of autonomous vehicles. The autonomous vehicle needs to be able to correctly distinguish between real objects that are obstacles from illusory ones. If the software, be it the AI algorithm or the programmed algorithm, cannot do this, then it ought not to be on public roads.

---

[237] Sean O'Kane, 'Uber reportedly thinks its self-driving car killed someone because it "decided" not to swerve', *The Verge* (7 May 2018) <https://www.theverge.com/2018/5/7/17327682/uber-self-driving-car-decision-kill-swerve> accessed 13 May 2018.

[238] Ibid.

[239] Ibid.

[240] Ibid.

Algorithm design and machine learning and its applicability to causing the Uber autonomous vehicle accident will be discussed further in Chapter 4.[241]

Autonomous vehicles must be able to detect and properly classify objects such as vehicles, pedestrians and fallen trees in its path but it must be able to distinguish these dangerous obstacles from a harmless plastic bag flying in front of it.

Contrary to the descriptions reported by some journalists, it may not be about 'tuning the software' in one direction or another. Some journalists have described the scenario inaccurately:[242]

> Software designers face a basic tradeoff here. If the software is programmed to be too cautious, the ride will be slow and jerky, as the car constantly slows down for objects that pose no threat to the car or aren't there at all. Tuning the software in the opposite direction will produce a smooth ride most of the time – but at the risk that the software will occasionally ignore a real object.

What these journalists have described is at the end stage of the decision-making process by the autonomous vehicle, and there is also a wrong assumption that an autonomous vehicle maker can or should have such a wide discretion in programming at that point in time.

3.7.5. No Infrared Sensor

At a very early stage of the process, the autonomous vehicle's devices and sensors should and must be able to correctly classify objects and obstacles, even if the classification is just about what kinds of materials the obstacle or object is made from, in which direction the object is moving, the velocity of the object and so on. What this means is that from the various sensors and devices, the autonomous vehicle should be able to correctly classify if an obstacle is made from metal, or is a warm-blooded creature like a human being or dog, or is a thin plastic bag, or a solid tree trunk. For any autonomous vehicle to be able to do this properly, it needs to have on-board multiple redundant overlapping detection systems.

In the accident that killed Herzberg, Uber's autonomous vehicle could not detect or classify Herzberg correctly as a human being.[243] Ideally, the informa-

---

[241] See Chapter 4, Section 4.3.4.2.

[242] Timothy B Lee, 'Report: Software bug led to death in Uber's self-driving crash', *Ars Technica* (8 May 2018) <https://arstechnica.com/tech-policy/2018/05/report-software-bug-led-to-death-in-ubers-self-driving-crash/> accessed 13 May 2018. See also Sean O'Kane (n 237).

[243] NTSB, *Preliminary Report Highway HWY18MH010* (n 212).

tion from its lidar and radars combined should have established this. However, when the essential devices to meet the standard of care are considered,[244] it seems that Uber is missing an infrared system.[245] As discussed above and in Chapter 2, infrared systems are a vital component in detecting humans and animals on the roads. Passive infrared vision detects differences in the heat emitted by objects. Warm-blooded humans and animals can be easily detected. Infrared systems provide visual information, as well as the two-dimensional shape of objects, and they do not require light to operate. They are in fact ideal for providing night vision to autonomous vehicles.[246]

Given that Uber's autonomous vehicle struck Herzberg at nighttime and it was not equipped with an infrared system, it could be argued that had the autonomous vehicle had on-board an infrared system, Herzberg would have been correctly classified as a human being and presumably, if Uber had programmed its autonomous vehicle to stop for human beings in its path, it would have applied the brakes and Herzberg would not have been killed.

The missing infrared system on the autonomous vehicle is also particularly relevant in this accident as Herzberg was pushing a bicycle, which presumably would have been made from metal. The lidar and radars on the autonomous vehicle may not have known how to deal with the combination of metal and human flesh moving together side by side in that manner, that is, without the human being on the bicycle itself. As a result, it may not have known how to classify this obstacle and presumed it was a false positive given that two different types of materials were detected moving together in a side-by-side unknown manner – unknown if the software on Uber's SUV was not programmed to recognize a human and metal moving together side by side and not with the human sitting on the bicycle. This would of course be a programming and algorithm shortcoming. However, if an infrared system had been utilized by Uber, then the autonomous vehicle would have received absolutely clear confirmation from the infrared system that the obstacle ahead is indeed a human being even though there is also a metal object moving along with it. From this classification that the obstacle is a human being, any reasonable autonomous vehicle manufacturer would program its vehicle to swerve or apply the brakes and the accident would have been prevented.

What the foregoing highlights is that the classification of obstacles does not need to and should not be left to AI algorithms, machine learning and prob-

---

[244] See above Section 3.2.

[245] See Heather Somerville, Paul Lienert and Alexandria Sage (n 222) for a full description of the sensors on Uber's SUVs.

[246] Mark Harris, 'Night vision for self-driving cars', *IEEE Spectrum* (18 October 2017) <https://spectrum.ieee.org/cars-that-think/transportation/self-driving/do-self driving-cars-need-night-vision> accessed 23 April 2018.

ability when there are sensors that can perform the classification confidently and with high accuracy. In this case, the relevant sensor is the infrared sensor, which unfortunately was missing on Uber's autonomous vehicle.

Since Uber's autonomous vehicle misclassified Herzberg, its lack of due care in omitting an infrared system on the autonomous vehicle rendered Uber to have fallen below the required standard of care in equipping its autonomous vehicle with all the necessary devices and sensors.

3.7.6.   Only One Safety Driver

The inward facing video clip of the accident just before Herzberg was hit revealed that Uber's safety driver inside the car was looking down just prior to the accident instead of monitoring the road. Her hands were also not hovering near the steering wheel, ready to take over in the event of an emergency.

In the Preliminary Report, Uber stated that its operator inside the autonomous vehicle is responsible for monitoring diagnostic messages that appear on an interface in the centre stack of the vehicle dash and tagging events of interest for subsequent review.[247] From the video clip of the interior of the vehicle, it appeared that the operator was looking down at her lap but the operator told investigators that she was looking at the system interface at the centre stack. The Preliminary Report also described the movement as 'the vehicle operator glancing down toward the center of the vehicle several times before the crash'.[248] It remains to be seen if the final report from NTSB will shed any further light on this. The significance is that, if indeed the safety driver was monitoring the system interface, then it is a design fault of Uber's, in terms of the location of the interface system. If the safety driver was looking down at a phone or something else on her lap, then she would have failed in her duties as a safety driver but questions remain as to whether the tasks given to her were reasonable.

Research has shown that humans monitoring an automated system are likely to become bored and disengaged,[249] fallible, distractable and, perhaps, easily seduced by machines that appear to function safely.[250] As a result of this, there is a temptation to look at mobile phones, fall asleep and otherwise not pay

---

[247]   NTSB, *Preliminary Report Highway HWY18MH010* (n 212).
[248]   Ibid.
[249]   Sam Levin (n 209).
[250]   Olivia Solon, 'Who's driving? Autonomous cars may be entering the most dangerous phase', *The Guardian* (24 January 2018) <https://www.theguardian.com/technology/2018/jan/24/self-driving-cars-dangerous-period-false-security> accessed 23 April 2018.

attention to the road ahead. Uber was well aware of this[251] but yet it did not take any actions to help prevent its safety driver from becoming bored and disengaged whilst inside the autonomous vehicle. Indeed, its decision in late 2017 to reduce the number of persons in the autonomous vehicles to only one may have exacerbated this.[252]

A second point to note is that reports indicated that Uber's autonomous vehicles required more frequent human intervention to steer the autonomous vehicle out of trouble, with Uber's autonomous vehicles having problems driving through construction zones and next to tall vehicles.[253] Uber's human drivers had to intervene far more frequently than the drivers of competing autonomous vehicles projects; for example, Waymo's autonomous vehicles were able to travel an average of nearly 5600 miles before the driver had to take control to steer the autonomous vehicle out of trouble but as at March 2018, Uber's autonomous vehicles were struggling to meet a target of 13 miles per human intervention.[254]

Despite its autonomous vehicles' poor performance at driving without human intervention, Uber still proceeded to reduce the number of safety drivers from two to one in late 2017.[255] This exacerbated the problem of the safety driver becoming bored and disengaged. Former safety drivers have maintained that it was difficult to remain alert through long hours with little stimulus.[256] A full-time employee is required to sit alert behind the wheel for 8–10 hours, with one scheduled 30 minute lunch break.[257] Workers were often assigned to repeat the same circuit over the course of their shift, in order to deeply familiarize the autonomous vehicle's self-driving technology with portions of the city which Uber has mapped.[258] The solitude and monotony of the repeated routes made it difficult for safety drivers to maintain focus.[259]

It is because of the inherent boredom and disengagement associated with the tasks performed by the safety driver that Uber's decision to remove the second

---

[251] Daisuke Wakabayashi, 'Uber's self-driving cars were struggling before Arizona crash', *The New York Times* (23 March 2018) <https://www.nytimes.com/2018/03/23/technology/uber-self-driving-cars-arizona.html?smid=tw-share> accessed 23 April 2018.

[252] Ibid.

[253] Ibid.

[254] Ibid.

[255] Ibid.

[256] Laura Bliss, 'Former Uber backup driver: "We saw this coming"', *Citylab* (27 March 2018) <https://www.citylab.com/transportation/2018/03/former-uber-backup-driver-we-saw-this-coming/556427/> accessed 13 May 2018.

[257] Ibid.

[258] Ibid.

[259] Ibid.

person in the test autonomous vehicles may not have been a sound decision as the second person played an indirect role in maintaining safety because the second person provided a source of stimulation for the safety driver as well as a second set of eyes to watch the road even if that was not their primary role. The situation is even more acute as Uber's autonomous vehicles required more constant human interventions than its competitors, indicating that the safety driver would be more fatigued by the increased interventions required but yet at the same time be tempted to be distracted and disengaged, even as the overall risk of Uber's autonomous vehicle needing to be steered out of trouble is higher than its competitors and hence it poses a greater danger for the general public.

One last point to note is that, if indeed the safety driver was monitoring the interface system, then Uber has also fallen short of its duty of care through its omission to employ a second person inside the autonomous vehicle to monitor the interface system. Driving is a task which requires the driver to be attentive to the roads at all times. This is so as the vehicle is a moving object, or even a moving weapon. Uber expected its safety drivers to take over driving in emergency situations; this cannot possibly be achieved if Uber also requires its safety drivers to monitor the interface system at the same time.

Given the circumstances in which Herzberg was killed, it is very likely that Uber fell below the required standard of care in having only one person inside its test autonomous vehicle for a number of different reasons. Uber could have taken a number of steps to mitigate the situation, such as changing the routes during each shift or having more frequent breaks, but it did not.[260]

3.8.   SUMMARY OF VERIFIABLE STANDARDS

This chapter has primarily focused on those aspects of regulating autonomous vehicles that can be verified, especially through material and physical sciences. From the properties of sensors and devices, it is possible to piece together what an autonomous vehicle is or is not capable of by examining the suite of sensors and devices it has on-board. This chapter has set out what would be the essential suite of sensors and devices an autonomous vehicle ought to have on-board in order to meet the standard of care owed to drivers and the general public as manufacturers of vehicles. It has tested this suite of sensors and devices against the accidents that have occurred involving autonomous vehicle and semi-autonomous vehicles to date.

---

[260]   Ibid. The comments of the former safety drivers are illuminating on the culture at Uber.

This chapter has also canvassed other non-device-related verifiable standards such as the requirement to disclose accidents, especially if the technology is still in the public beta-testing stage; confusing or misleading conduct and statements about the autonomous vehicle's functions and capabilities; and the required due care of safety drivers and the conditions under which they operate autonomous vehicles.

4. Software: difficult to verify standards of care

Chapter 3 has discussed those required standards of care that are easy to verify because they are based on the physical or material sciences and/or they are taken from existing negligence law which guides what would be regarded as right behaviour. This chapter deals with the more difficult issue of setting standards of care for those aspects of autonomous vehicles that cannot be easily verified because they are software based, whether as hard-coded software, or as AI algorithms.

4.1. HARD-CODED SOFTWARE

Hard-coded software can, technically speaking, be traced so as to follow each step that the programming code takes, which any software programmer can debug if they are given access to all of the programming code. Debugging is the term for the technical process of weeding out the bugs or problems in the programming code which cause it to function other than as intended. A simple example of this might be a program to add up 10 numbers. If the result of the program does not give the right answer when compared with a manual addition, a software programmer can go through the programming code, line by line, to determine what went wrong. The bug in the computer program could be as simple as the original computer programmer using the multiplication sign instead of the addition sign in the computer program algorithm for the calculation.

In this sense, it is possible to verify whether hard-coded software has met the standard of care of a reasonable person in the shoes of the computer programmer. A simple example might be if the programming code is written such that, if an autonomous vehicle encounters a set of traffic lights, and the traffic lights are red, the programming code still instructs the autonomous vehicle to accelerate. This would be a clear breach of the standard of care. The computer program should, of course, instruct the autonomous vehicle to stop in the event of meeting a red traffic light. This would meet the required standard of care.

From the foregoing, it should be evident how critical it is for the objects on the road to be properly sensed. The central computer program would need firm confirmation from its sensors and devices that the object in front of it is a traffic light and that the light is indeed red, then it can program the autonomous vehicle to stop.

The importance of this is played out in Uber's autonomous vehicle that killed Elaine Herzberg. Uber stated that its autonomous vehicle required the human safety driver to intervene in emergency situations to apply the brakes.[1] Not all autonomous vehicle companies rely entirely on a safety driver to apply the brakes in a crisis as some use the autonomous system itself to apply the brakes.[2] However, in order to be able to do this, the autonomous system must be very confident of what the object in front of the autonomous vehicle is. Otherwise, the autonomous system would be applying the brakes for flying paper bags and other items that it need not avoid. Uber's explanation as to why it switched off the emergency braking system seems to suggest that this was exactly what was happening when its SUVs were being tested; Uber said that it disabled the emergency braking system 'to reduce the potential for erratic vehicle behaviour'.[3] This seems to indicate that Uber's SUV was often mistaking harmless objects for obstacles it must avoid, hence the persistent trigger of the emergency braking systems, often resulting in erratic vehicle behaviour. All of this points to the very high possibility that Uber's autonomous vehicle technology is immature.

To be clear, in the technical sense, while it is possible for hard-coded software to be verified, it requires a lot of time and diligent software programmers to trace the programming code. Between the autonomous vehicle developer and any regulator, the onus of proof should fall on the developers of the autonomous system as the developers should be the ones who should be held accountable if the software program is found to contain bugs or programming instructions contrary to what a reasonable and prudent person would program (such as accelerating through a red traffic light). This is, of course, a stance very different from much software that is available in the mass consumer market today, such as operating systems and word processing software, whereby the software developer contracts out of liability and there is very little regulatory oversight.

Whilst pinning the responsibility and liability on the developer of the autonomous system may set a standard of care that is on par with general negligence law, it does not assist with the question of whether governments should allow

---

[1]   NTSB, *Preliminary Report Highway HWY18MH010* <https://www.ntsb.gov/investigations/AccidentReports/Reports/HWY18MH010-prelim.pdf> accessed 30 May 2018, 2.

[2]   Tim Bradshaw and Shannon Bond, 'Self-driving car crash report highlights Uber safety shortcomings', *Financial Times* (25 May 2018) <https://www.ft.com/content/2c3d8efc-5fb2-11e8-9334-2218e7146b04> accessed 28 May 2018, 2.

[3]   NTSB, *Preliminary Report Highway HWY18MH010* (n 1).

autonomous vehicles on the roads, even at the testing stage, and what safe-guards should be in place to protect the general public who use the roads.

At a general level, hard-coded software is difficult to verify in the sense that it is extremely time-consuming and tedious to verify and difficult to obtain access to all of the programming code. Unlike sensors and other devices on an autonomous vehicle, computer program code is not publicly visible or acces-sible, and in any event, since computer software is protected under copyright law in many countries, most software developers would not want to make their computer program code available as it forms part of their intellectual property and is proprietary material. This poses a number of practical problems.

From a regulator's point of view, while it could require all of the program-ming code to be made available to it for the purposes of testing and certifi-cation, it is not feasible for a regulator to work through possibly millions of lines of programming code on an autonomous vehicle to verify that it has been properly programmed to be safe and fit to be on public roads. Even if the reg-ulator placed the burden of proof on the manufacturer of autonomous vehicles to demonstrate how every line of the programming code functions and how all of the pieces of the programming code work together, including the machine learning algorithms, this would still be extremely time-consuming for the reg-ulator and there is still no certainty that the software would function as claimed without the regulator working through the entire computer program itself.

Between the developer of autonomous vehicles and a plaintiff, not only would a plaintiff face the same impossibility of working through millions of lines of programming code, but it would also be even harder for any plaintiff to extract the entire source code of the program from the developer.

4.2.   AI ALGORITHMS – MACHINE LEARNING

As discussed in Chapter 2, in addition to hard-coded programming code, much of the decision-making on autonomous vehicles relies on AI algorithms and machine learning. The level of AI algorithms and machine learning on autonomous vehicles will differ from vehicle to vehicle. How the suite of sensors are integrated with the software will also differ from manufacturer to manufacturer. Even how much hard-coded programming code is involved and how it interfaces with AI algorithms will depend on each developer.

The following sections will briefly explain how AI algorithms and machine learning function, with particular reference to autonomous vehicles.

4.2.1.   What is Machine Learning

In a hard-coded computer program, the programmer will need to manually code in a programming language what the program will do for every possible scenario at every step of the process. It is therefore possible to build an entire AI machine without using machine learning at all, but this would require writing millions of lines of codes with complex rules and decision-trees. For a developer of an autonomous vehicle or any autonomous system, decisions need to be made on how much work should be done by hard-coded software programs and how much work should be done by machine learning or AI algorithms.

There is no set formula as to what and how much of the computer program should be hard-coded, but to meet standards of care, rules such as ensuring that the autonomous vehicle stops at a red traffic light and stops at a stop sign should probably be hard-coded and not left to machine learning, lest the machine-learning algorithm makes catastrophic mistakes at a road intersection.

4.2.2.   Statistical Learning

At a very general level, machine learning is where computers have the ability to execute functions without being explicitly programmed to do so. Loosely speaking, instead of hard-coding line by line specific instructions to accomplish a particular task, machine learning is a way of 'training' an algorithm so that it can learn. To be clear, the algorithm does not actually learn in the way that human beings learn.[4] This is a way of describing what the process involves. In essence, the process involves the design and implementation of computer programs that detect patterns in data. A more accurate term to describe the process would be 'statistical learning'.[5]

Bayes' theorem and his ideas about probability as a measure of belief underlie much of modern AI technology, and this should be at the forefront of considerations for any decisions made on standards of care and regulation. A machine learning program will typically comprise data, mathematical models and algorithms to determine the decision to be made. Machine learning is essentially data analysis that automates the building of analytical models. The process is simplistically described as systems or machines learning from data, identifying patterns and making decisions with minimal human intervention. For the machine to be 'trained' or to 'learn', the algorithm is fed huge amounts of data and often the algorithm can be allowed to adjust itself and improve.

---

[4]   Ian H Witten, *Data Mining: Practical Machine Learning Tools and Techniques* (3rd edn, Elsevier 2011), § 1.3.

[5]   Prakash Nadkarni, *Clinical Research Computing* (Elsevier 2016), ch 4.

Machine learning is not a new technology and many machine-learning algorithms have been in use for a long time.[6] Machine learning stemmed from pattern recognition and the ability of computers and software to be iterative. Recent developments in computational power and the ability to automatically apply complex mathematical calculations to big data repeatedly and with high speed have propelled machine learning and AI algorithms to new heights. The iterative aspect of machine learning enables the mathematical models to independently adapt as they are exposed to new data. The previous computations enable the models to produce more or less reliable, repeatable decisions and results.

Machine learning is essentially an algorithm or model that detects patterns in data and then predicts similar patterns in new data utilizing a lot of complex mathematics and statistics. The mathematics and the mathematical models produced are the drivers of the algorithm, so they need to be soundly constructed, although many general mathematical modelling tools have become available commercially.[7] The mathematics utilized aside, the algorithms also depend heavily on the data that have been fed to them.

Taking the example of stopping the autonomous vehicle at a red traffic light, this can be hard-coded into the computer software, so that the programming algorithm might look like this: if there is a red traffic light in front of the autonomous vehicle, then the autonomous vehicle should apply the brakes. This can also be achieved by a machine learning algorithm that examines a set of data where a human driver stops the vehicle 1000 times, in order to find a pattern as to why the human driver stopped the vehicle. The pattern that the algorithm might find is that in 800 of those times where the human driver stopped the vehicle, there was a traffic light and the traffic light was red. In this sense, the software has 'learnt' a rule from having found the pattern, the rule being that, if there is a red traffic light, then the brakes should be applied.

The algorithm might also find that, on 180 occasions out of the dataset of 1000 where the human driver stopped the vehicle, there was a Stop sign. Depending on the mathematical model used, the algorithm may find that 180 out of 1000 is not a statistically or sufficiently high occurrence and hence is not a pattern to be recognized, and it will thus not necessarily incorporate this as a rule to learn. As a result, it will not have 'learnt' any rule to apply the brakes when there is a Stop sign.

---

[6]   Stuart Russell and Peter Novig, *Artificial Intelligence: A Modern Approach* (3rd edn, Pearson 2010), ch 1.

[7]   See for example SAS <https://www.sas.com> and MATLAB <https://au.mathworks.com/products/matlab.html> accessed 23 May 2018.

From this simple example, it should be obvious that, although the machine 'learns', much of this 'learning' is dependent on the dataset involved, the quantity in the dataset and what kinds of algorithms have been used. If the dataset is too small, it will not learn the desired rule.

Machine learning can be of four types: supervised, unsupervised, semi-supervised and reinforcement learning. These will now be considered.

4.2.2.1. Supervised machine learning

Supervised machine learning is where the desired outcome is known, such as the rule to stop the autonomous vehicle at a red traffic light. The learning algorithm is fed a set of labelled inputs along with the corresponding correct outputs, and the algorithm learns by comparing its actual output with correct outputs to find errors. With each iteration, the algorithm modifies the model accordingly. Supervised learning algorithms try to find a formula that accurately predicts the output label from input variables. This can be done through techniques such as linear and logistic regression, and multi-class classification. In all of these, the goal is the construction of a succinct model that can predict the value of the output from the attribute variables. The only difference is that for regression, the output is a numerical value and for multi-class classification, the output is categorical. The model construction continues until the statistical model or formula achieves a low probability of error.[8]

Returning to the example of stopping at a red traffic light, the input data may comprise labelled inputs that may contain a few variables, such as red lights, and the actions taken of accelerate, apply brakes or do nothing. The labelled inputs for apply brakes would be labelled as the correct action. When these are fed to the algorithm, the algorithm will detect this pattern and produce a formula that will provide the answer or prediction of apply brakes whenever there is a red traffic light. Supervised learning is commonly used in applications where historical data predicts likely future events. So in this example, historical data of applying the brakes at a red traffic light predicts the future event of applying the brakes, which would, in an autonomous vehicle, be translated into an instruction to apply the brakes.

4.2.2.2. Unsupervised machine learning

Unsupervised machine learning is where the system is not given the 'right answer' – the input data is not labelled. The algorithm must detect the pattern on its own and try to derive a value from the available data. Generally, the goal is to explore the data and develop a relation within the data, in order to detect the patterns or to divide the dataset into categories or subgroups depending on

---

[8]   Stuart Russell and Peter Novig (n 6).

the level of similarity between them. Some of the more common techniques for unsupervised machine learning include clustering and association rule learning.[9]

Using the same example of stopping at the red traffic light, unsupervised machine learning would entail the algorithm being fed data that has no labels, and there should be more data samples with vehicles applying the brakes at a red traffic light in the dataset in order for the algorithm to learn. It is evident then that, if in the event the dataset contains more data samples of applying the accelerator at a red traffic light, then this will be the pattern that the algorithm will detect and it will be the rule which the algorithm will learn. It is thus essential that the dataset is an accurate reflection of how one wishes the autonomous vehicle to behave. Unsupervised machine learning can be used for image recognition, such as in situations where the algorithm is learning to detect Stop signs which may be faded, or have been defaced, or in bad weather conditions.

4.2.2.3. Semi-supervised machine learning

Semi-supervised machine learning is similar to supervised learning except that the data for training include both labelled and unlabelled data. This method has the advantage that unlabelled data is less expensive and takes less effort to acquire

4.2.2.4. Reinforcement machine learning

In reinforcement machine learning, the algorithm discovers through trial and error which actions yield the greatest rewards[10] – in technical terms, these rewards are termed time-delayed and sparse labels.[11] Reinforcement machine learning comprises the agent, the environment and actions. The agent is the learner or decision-maker, the environment is what the agent interacts with and actions are what the agent can do. The aim is for the agent to choose actions that maximize the rewards. The rules for how the agent chooses those actions are called policy. So, in order for the agent to maximize rewards, it needs to learn the best policy.[12] From the foregoing, it is not surprising that reinforcement machine learning is often used for robotics, gaming[13] and navigation.

---

[9]   Ibid, ch 20.
[10] Ibid, ch 21.
[11] Tambet Matiisen, 'Demystifying deep reinforcement learning' (19 December 2015) <http://neuro.cs.ut.ee/demystifying-deep-reinforcement-learning/> accessed 23 May 2018.
[12] Ibid.
[13] Volodymyr Mnih et al, 'Playing atari with deep reinforcement learning', arXiv: 1312.5602 (19 December 2013) <http://arxiv.org/abs/1312.5602> accessed 23 May 2018.

An easy to understand example of the application of reinforcement learning on autonomous vehicles would be its use in controlling the autonomous vehicle's steering wheel. Whilst lidars and cameras may detect lane markings on the road and help steer the steering wheel, there can be problems if the lane markings are non-existent or faded, such as in Walter Huang's Tesla crash. Reinforcement learning may also be used as a feedback loop even where the lane markings are clear and fine. For example, on a slightly curved road, rewards can be given to the algorithm if there are no sudden jerky motions of steering the autonomous vehicle away from a lane-marking line. This can help the algorithm learn what are the rules and best policy to keep the autonomous vehicle within its lane at all times without sudden movements. To be clear, reinforcement learning algorithms in this regard is still in its infancy.[14]

In reinforcement machine learning, how the agent learns to behave in an environment depends on the rewards. This means that the rewards have to be properly defined or set. If rewards are missing, or if the rewards are awarded wrongly, this will adversely affect the reinforcement machine learning.

4.2.2.5. Neural networks and deep learning

It is important at this juncture to raise the issue of neural networks. There is much hype concerning neural networks and deep learning. Deep learning is, very generally speaking, machine learning algorithms that are designed and structured in multiple levels or layers and are interconnected, resembling a neural network architecture.[15]

Much deep learning utilizes multi-layered artificial neural networks. Neural networks are often described as mimicking the brain with many layers and with weighted interconnected nodes and branches that are hidden and where the actual processing is done. They are often represented as necessary 'black boxes' where only the input and outputs are known and the calculations are so complex and so cleverly processed inside the neural network that no one knows how it derives the outputs.[16] This reads more like a page taken from a science fiction book. In truth, no software needs to be a 'black box'. Every single processing step undertaken by a computer program, including those utilizing machine learning algorithms, can be visibly displayed. All that is needed is for the computer programmer to add a line of code at every step to

---

[14] Simon Kardell and Mattias Kuosku, 'Autonomous vehicle control via deep reinforcement learning' (Master's thesis, Chalmers University of Technology 2017) <http://publications.lib.chalmers.se/records/fulltext/252902/252902.pdf> accessed 23 May 2018.

[15] Gary Marcus, 'Deep learning: A critical appraisal', arXiv:1801.00631 [cs.AI] (2 January 2018) <https://arxiv.org/abs/1801.00631> accessed 23 May 2018.

[16] Ibid.

display the step and whatever values are in that step, whether input or output. The display can be to the computer screen, or to print to a file.

Whilst there have been spectacular successes reported in the press about deep learning and neural networks,[17] the popular press does not report the spectacular failures. Nor does the popular press generally ask the question of whether the spectacular success is somehow confined or limited in scope or applicability. For example, when AlphaGo Zero mastered the board game Go without human help, it made headline news internationally.[18] Whilst the achievement itself is significant, many did not stop to consider what was unique about this so-called breakthrough that enabled the AlphaGo Zero algorithm to perform so well. For a start, the board game Go is after all just a board game. It has rules. Those rules were fed to the algorithm. Computers function best in structured settings such as where there are rules. Computers are also excellent at processing millions of iterations in one second. No human brain can beat that. Thus, it comes as no surprise that in a well-structured board game with set rules the algorithm is able to perform well.

Some experts have also echoed that the success of AlphaGo Zero is limited to a very unrealistic problem because it is a completely self-contained problem in that there is no variability and it is deterministic.[19] There are a limited number of possibilities in a game of Go compared with many real-world environments.[20] Many real-world problems (such as navigation) take place in partially observable and non-deterministic environments.[21] Experts doubt that AlphaGo Zero's success will make much significant impact on real-world applications and view it as more of an academic achievement.[22]

One of the most spectacular failures of neural networks can be found in a research paper published in 2015 which showed how easy it was for

[17]   For example, Ian Sample, 'It's able to create knowledge itself: Google unveils AI that learns on its own', *The Guardian* (18 October 2017) <https://www.theguardian .com/science/2017/oct/18/its-able-to-create-knowledge-itself-google-unveils-ai-learns -all-on-its-own> accessed 23 May 2018.
[18]   Ibid. See also David Meyer, 'Google's new AlphaGo breakthrough could take algorithms where no humans have gone', *Fortune* (19 October 2017) <http://fortune .com/2017/10/19/google-alphago-zero-deepmind-artificial-intelligence/> accessed 23 May 2018.
[19]   Nick Heath, 'AI: How big a deal is Google's latest AlphaGo breakthrough?', *TechRepublic* (3 November 2017) <https://www.techrepublic.com/article/ai-how-big-a -deal-is-googles-latest-alphago-breakthrough/> accessed 23 May 2018.
[20]   Ibid.
[21]   Ibid.
[22]   Ibid.

researchers to trick neural networks.[23] In this research, the researchers tested the reliability of state-of-the-art deep neural networks in recognizing objects. The researchers evolved regular images to form abstract ones and tested them on deep neural networks. The results were laughable; amongst some of the research results, the deep neural networks classified yellow and black horizontal stripes as a school bus without any need to have a windscreen or wheels or any other characteristics of a real bus. Vertical zig-zagged red stripes against a white background were classified by the state-of-the-art deep neural network with 99.6% certainty as a baseball.[24] There are also other failures of neural networks that appear in academic journals but which do not make it to headline news.[25]

In December 2017, researchers at Berkeley published new research that used physical adversarial examples to test the YOLO detector, a popular state-of-the-art algorithm with good real-time performance that utilizes neural networks. The researchers stuck various stickers to a real physical Stop sign.[26] They tested the YOLO neural network from different angles and recorded videos, and the YOLO neural network did not perceive the Stop sign in almost all of the frames until the camera was around 3–4 feet away from it, which is extremely close. In real life, if an autonomous vehicle was only a few feet away from a Stop sign before it recognized it, the autonomous vehicle would be too close to take effective corrective action, such as apply the brakes, without overshooting into the intersection and possibly causing an accident. The researchers also tested the adversarial examples against another neural network, Faster-RCNN and the results were also the same: that the Stop sign was detected only when the camera was 3–4 feet away.[27]

---

[23]   Anh Nguyen, Jason Yosinski and Jeff Clune, 'Deep neural networks are easily fooled: High confidence predictions for unrecognizable images' in Computer Vision and Pattern Recognition (CVPR '15) (IEEE 2015). Also available for download at <http://www.evolvingai.org/files/DNNsEasilyFooled_cvpr15.pdf> accessed 23 May 2018.

[24]   Ibid.

[25]   El Mahdi El Mhamdi and Rachid Guerraoui, 'When neurons fail', arXiv:1706 .08884v1 (27 June 2017) <https://arxiv.org/pdf/1706.08884.pdf> accessed 23 May 2018.

[26]   Ivan Evtimov, Kevin Eykholt, Earlence Fernandes and Bo Li, 'Physical adversarial examples against deep neural networks', *Berkeley Artificial Intelligence Research* (30 December 2017) <http://bair.berkeley.edu/blog/2017/12/30/yolo-attack/> accessed 23 May 2018.

[27]   For further examples of neural network failures, see Tom Simonite, 'AI has a hallucination problem that's proving tough to fix', *Wired* (9 March 2018) <https: //www.wired.com/story/ai-has-a-hallucination-problem-thats-proving-tough-to-fix/> accessed 23 May 2018.

The point of this discussion on deep learning and neural networks is to present a balanced view. Far too much hype has been presented by the popular media and some developers themselves. Professor Marcus has aptly summed up the current situation:[28]

> The real problem lies in misunderstanding what deep learning is, and is not, good for. The technique excels at solving closed-end classification problems, in which a wide range of potential signals must be mapped onto a limited number of categories, given that there is enough data available and the test set closely resembles the training set.

In terms of the utility of deep learning and neural networks for autonomous vehicles, one critical point must be made. No manufacturer of autonomous vehicles should utilize neural networks or deep learning unless they have full knowledge of the processes and algorithms inside them. It would be completely unacceptable under the law of negligence to simply assert that the neural network is a black box should anything go amiss. The manufacturer of autonomous vehicles must show due care in the development of autonomous vehicles. This means that they must at the very least know and understand the algorithms utilized on their vehicles. Failure in this regard would mean a certain breach of the standard of care owed to the drivers of its autonomous vehicles as well as to other road users.

4.3.   STANDARDS OF CARE

4.3.1.   Hard-coded Software – Normal Driving Conditions

As already discussed in Section 4.1 above, software can be hard-coded, and this can be traced, but this is time-consuming and tedious and one would need access to all of the original lines of programming source code. The onus of proving that the standard of care has been met should fall on the manufacturers of autonomous vehicles and they should not be allowed to contract out of liability owing to the sophisticated nature of autonomous vehicles and the great harm they can cause.

The baseline standards of care for hard-coded software can be gleaned from the existing traffic rules and what a prudent driver would do in the circumstances. Hence, for normal straightforward driving conditions, the autonomous vehicle should be programmed to stop at red traffic lights, stop at Stop signs, give way to oncoming traffic if turning and so on. Any hard-coded software

---

[28]   Gary Marcus (n 15), 15.

that is contrary to traffic rules should be deemed to have breached the standard of care.

This deals with the question of liability between the manufacturer and road users, including the driver of the autonomous vehicle. There still remains the practical difficulties for plaintiffs to gain access to the entire software programming code and to have the resources to work through the millions of lines of programming code necessary to discover breaches. It also leaves the bigger question of whether autonomous vehicles and semi-autonomous vehicles should be allowed on public roads, during the testing stage and beyond, and what safeguards regulators should impose. These issues will be discussed in Chapter 6.

4.3.2. Hard-coded Software – Difficult Cases

There will be difficult cases if and when software is hard-coded, such as requiring the computer programmer to make a choice of taking one of several possible actions, all of which are harmful but some causing more harm than others, for example, the classic 'trolley problem' of whether to kill one person or to kill five people. The standard of care for difficult cases will be discussed in Chapter 6 on ethics.

4.3.3. Apportionment of Hard-coding and Machine Learning Algorithms

There is no set formula as to what and how much of the autonomous vehicle software should be hard-coded and what and how much could be left to machine learning algorithms. To be clear, it is possible to have almost the entire function of an autonomous vehicle hard-coded but this would mean many more millions of lines of programming code comprising many permutations and many decision trees, which would make the software massive and clunky and not terribly efficient to run.

By and large, developers will develop their own software engineering design strategies in line with the devices and sensors they have on-board. Some critical functions should probably be hard-coded and not left to machine learning. Critical functions would include those that may cause serious harm, such as not stopping at a red traffic light and not stopping when the obstacle in front of the autonomous vehicle is warm-blooded, whether a human being or a dog or some other creature. As a matter of general safety, autonomous vehicle manufacturers should ensure that these critical functions are hard-coded, failing which they may find themselves not meeting the required standard of care should harm occur. For a plaintiff and for the regulator, the difficulties already highlighted for hard-coded software are also relevant here.[29]

4.3.4.   Machine Learning Algorithms

The foregoing sections have elucidated that machine learning is in effect statistical learning based on probability theorems. Being statistical learning, there is very little substantive reasoning, like human reasoning, behind the machine learning. Indeed, as one commentator has noted, it is 'intelligent results without intelligence'.[30] This fact should always be borne in mind in any regulation and any setting of standards of care.

From the various forms of machine learning discussed above,[31] it should be highlighted that all of the input that the developers feed the algorithms, that is, the 'training', will affect how well or how poorly the algorithms function. This has serious ramifications for trying to determine what ought to be the standard of care.

4.3.4.1. Size of the datasets
For starters, the size of the datasets fed to the algorithms to train them needs to be substantially large. If a machine learning algorithm has only had a few examples of a phenomenon fed to it from which to detect relevant patterns, it will perform poorly. In many cases, the machine learning algorithm will require many hundreds of thousands of examples of the relevant phenomenon in order to produce a useful and robust set of predictive models. To be clear, a dataset of 1000 examples would very likely be quite insufficient for an algorithm to be trained properly and to yield sound results in most cases.

There is no set magical number of samples in a dataset beyond the threshold at which one can definitively declare that the machine algorithm has been properly trained. Furthermore, the size of the required training dataset will differ depending on the task. Some tasks will have fewer variations than others and can master the task with a smaller training dataset. Of course, if an autonomous vehicle has only used 100 samples in its training datasets for all functions, it will clearly be insufficiently trained and it will not have met the standard of care owed to the general public and to its drivers. Beyond that, unlike hard-coded software, it will be extremely difficult to ascertain whether

---

[29] See Section 4.3.1.
[30] Harry Surden, 'Machine learning and law' (2014) 89 Washington Law Review 87, 95.
[31] See Section 4.2.

a sufficiently large training dataset has been fed to the algorithm so that the standard of care has been met.

It is for this reason that, for each function of an autonomous vehicle, the manufacturer needs to continue to conduct many test drives, since the vehicles are also collecting data during the test drives to train other autonomous vehicles that the manufacturer has on the roads. There are also publicly available datasets that can be used for training autonomous vehicle algorithms.[32] It must, however, be noted that a dataset may contain one hour of driving data, but within that one hour of driving, 95 per cent of the time the vehicle may have been on a straight highway with little variation in the driving environment and clear conditions. There may have only been one traffic light encountered and no pedestrians or cyclists visible during the entire drive. If all of the training datasets were like this, then thousands of such datasets would not be helpful to the machine learning algorithm.

In March 2018, Baidu released an enormous dataset that is believed to be the largest open-source self-driving dataset publicly available.[33] The dataset, named ApolloScape, includes 26 pre-defined semantic items such as cars, bicycles, trucks, buildings, people and traffic lights.[34]

The manufacturers of autonomous vehicles rely on something called a confidence interval, which is designed to evaluate the mathematical model that has been constructed in terms of errors. Therefore, it is essentially a measure of the confidence in the prediction, for example, the probability that this particular mathematical model and algorithm is correct in predicting that the obstacle ahead is not moving and the autonomous vehicle will crash into it if the autonomous vehicle does not swerve or stop.

The problem with using such measures as objective criteria for evaluation is that such frameworks are dependent on the assumptions that the computer programmer has made, including the parameters that will determine the con-

---

[32]   Hang Yin and Christian Berger, 'When to use what data set for your self-driving car algorithm: An overview of publicly available driving datasets', *Researchgate* (October 2017) <https://www.researchgate.net/publication/320475411_When_to_use_what_data_set_for_your_self-driving_car_algorithm_An_overview_of_publicly_available_driving_datasets> accessed 23 May 2018.

[33]   Pranav Dar, 'Baidu has released a gigantic self-driving dataset named ApolloScape', *Analytics Vidhya* (19 March 2018) <https://www.analyticsvidhya.com/blog/2018/03/baidu-apollo-released-gigantic-self-driving-dataset/> accessed 23 May 2018.

[34]   See ApolloScape <http://apolloscape.auto/scene.html#to_general_href> accessed 23 May 2018.

fidence intervals and probabilities.[35] Hence, objectively, they are not a sound method of evaluation.

From the foregoing, it is evident that there will be difficulties for any party such as a plaintiff or a regulator in determining what is a good and appropriate dataset size in order to effectively train the machine learning algorithm to a level that will satisfy the standard of care.

4.3.4.2. Quality of the datasets

There are many issues of quality related to datasets. For the purposes here, only three will be considered because they will be sufficient to illustrate the challenges.

First, as alluded to in the preceding section, if the datasets used for training are all very similar with little variation in conditions that reflect those that could reasonably be encountered in real-life driving, then even thousands of such datasets will not help the machine learning algorithm learn effectively. The datasets must contain sufficient samples of the different variables in order for the machine learning algorithm to learn.

Second, the datasets need to be 'correct' or at least to represent acceptable behaviour. For example, for supervised machine learning, the data samples need to be correctly labelled. If large proportions of the training dataset for supervised machine learning are incorrectly labelled before they are fed to the algorithm, this will result in the algorithm either not learning or learning the wrong rules and constructing wrong models. As a concrete example, if the datasets contain predominantly vehicles speeding through red traffic lights labelled as correct, this will result in the algorithm learning that speeding through red traffic lights is a pattern to adopt. This can also occur in unsupervised machine learning. If the dataset is skewed such that there are more samples of vehicles speeding through red traffic lights, the algorithm will detect this pattern and will adopt it as one of its rules.

Third, the datasets need to have semantic segmentation properly applied to the training set before any machine learning can occur. Semantic segmentation enables the computer program to recognize and understand what is in the image at the pixel level. For a human being, it is second nature to detect if something is a person, a bicycle, a dog and so on. For the computer to perceive whether something is a human, the algorithm needs to be shown many images of what a human looks like. The algorithm can be told that a human has two legs but a long skirt worn by a woman may make her two legs look like one to

---

[35] Caitlin Hayes, 'How do you predict uncertainty in statistics and machine learning?', *Cornell CIS* <https://www.cis.cornell.edu/how-do-you-predict-uncertainty -statistics-and-machine-learning> accessed 23 May 2018.

the algorithm. In order to assist the algorithm, the datasets that are fed to the algorithm will need to be highlighted in different colours so that the algorithm can identify all of the humans, cats, dogs, road signs, traffic lights, buildings, bicycles and so on in the image.[36] This is called semantic segmentation. This is a painstaking task and if there are any mistakes, such as when human beings are wrongly labelled as tree trunks, this will adversely affect what the algorithm learns.

In the Uber autonomous vehicle crash that killed a pedestrian, the vehicle had 'classified the pedestrian as an unknown object, as a vehicle, and then as a bicycle with varying expectations of future travel path'.[37] The failure to classify the pedestrian as a pedestrian, either immediately or on subsequent iterations, has led experts to conclude that it is 'completely foreseeable that a person would be walking a bike across a street. They should have had that in their test data set before they went on a public road'.[38] This allegation is a clear indication that the quality of Uber's training dataset for its autonomous vehicles did not meet the required standard of care. Further, experts also said that this failure to classify the pedestrian as a pedestrian 'showed the limitations of machine learning systems, which rely on spotting patterns that have been repeatedly shown to the sensors'.[39]

From the foregoing, it should be apparent that, given the volume of data required and the necessity for all the datasets to be of a certain quality, these are fairly high thresholds that the autonomous vehicle manufacturer will need to be able to establish that they have met. Even harder still, if not impossible, will be for a plaintiff or the regulator to discover whether all of the data training datasets were indeed high-quality data training sets.

4.4.   CONCLUDING THOUGHTS ON STANDARDS OF CARE FOR SOFTWARE

This chapter has analysed how the software on autonomous vehicles functions, both in the form of hard-coded software as well as utilizing machine learning algorithms. In terms of both kinds of software methods, the architecture of each presents high hurdles for autonomous vehicle manufacturers to meet when guidance is taken from the current standards of care required under negligence law. Hard-coding software is tedious and time-consuming but it must

---

[36]   Jack Stewart, 'Mighty AI and the human army using phones to teach AI to drive', *Wired* (9 July 2017) <https://www.wired.com/story/mighty-ai-training-self-driving-cars/> accessed 23 May 2018.
[37]   NTSB, *Preliminary Report Highway HWY18MH010* (n 1).
[38]   Tim Bradshaw and Shannon Bond (n 2).
[39]   Ibid.

be done with due care and properly. A machine learning algorithm, although itself mathematically sound, is to a large extent heavily dependent on the data it has been trained on, which in turn raises issues concerning the quantity and quality of the datasets, the duration of the training and the parameters and input variables the computer programmers have designed. Moreover, the difficulties for a plaintiff or a regulator to establish whether there has been a breach of standard of care, whether with respect to hard-coded software or machine learning algorithms, reach the magnitude of impossibility.

An autonomous vehicle is not like a desktop computer operating system, which the general public has grown accustomed to containing bugs and security flaws. An autonomous vehicle is a moving object which can be deadly, not just for the driver but also for the general public. For this reason, the developers and manufacturers of autonomous vehicles must be held to a standard of care that meets high safety standards.

The question remains of how best this can be achieved so that lives are not unnecessarily lost. While many autonomous vehicle manufacturers and developers may be willing to strive to make autonomous vehicles a reality, the larger question remains of the role of the regulator in encouraging this kind of innovation but at the same time protect its citizens from injury, harm and death. These issues will be expounded in Chapter 5.

5.   The road less travelled for regulators

Chapter 3 has demonstrated the baseline suite of sensors and devices required on autonomous vehicles to ensure that they are able to sense their surroundings adequately. The manufacturers of autonomous vehicles should implement these in order to satisfy the standard of care owed to road users, including the drivers of its autonomous vehicles.

Chapter 4 has analysed the architecture of software on autonomous vehicles, both in the form of hard-coded software and in the form of machine learning algorithms. The bar for meeting the requisite standard of care for the developers and manufacturers of autonomous vehicles is high, and in the event of harm, the developers and manufacturers should be held accountable.

An important question that must be resolved is the responsibilities of the regulator, such as governments, in ensuring the technology is safe, safely tested and safely deployed, so that the citizenry is not harmed. As already elucidated in Chapter 1, many of the claims concerning autonomous vehicles being safer than human driven cars are more hype rather than reality.

The standards argued in Chapter 3 are relatively easy for regulators to mandate, and relatively easy for regulators to ensure compliance through checking. The software aspects canvassed in Chapter 4, however, raise hurdles, some which may not be easily overcome at the present time, if ever.

5.1.   HARD CODED SOFTWARE

A regulator can mandate all the programming code of an autonomous vehicle to be made available to it for the purposes of testing and certification, ignoring any protests of copyright and trade secrets protection. However, it is simply not feasible for regulators to work through possibly millions of lines of programming code for each autonomous vehicle to verify that it has been properly programmed to be safe and fit to have on public roads.

Not only would this be an onerous burden on the regulator, but it would require teams of highly skilled software engineers skilled in the area of autonomous vehicles. For a plaintiff, the difficulties in this regard are even higher as plaintiffs would usually have even fewer resources than a regulator.

5.2.   MACHINE LEARNING ALGORITHMS

The machine learning algorithms used on autonomous vehicles can be of any of the following four types: supervised, unsupervised, semi-supervised and reinforcement learning. Within each type of machine learning, many techniques can be applied to derive the algorithms and mathematical models.[1] All of these require complex mathematical and statistical methodologies, such as linear and logistic regression, classification and clustering.[2] It is inconceivable that any regulator would be able to hire enough highly specialized personnel skilled in such areas to evaluate all of the algorithms used in an autonomous vehicle. On any given autonomous vehicle, there could be hundreds of algorithms used for different functions. When the issue of quantity of datasets used as training data is considered, as was expounded in Chapter 4,[3] it is not possible to objectively determine what is a good and appropriate dataset size in order to effectively train the machine learning algorithm to a level that will satisfy the standard of care.

   Another difficult area for any regulator is evaluating the quality of the training datasets.[4] Given the voluminous amounts of data that is required to be fed to a machine learning algorithm, it is simply not possible for the regulator to check that every set of training data was without error in labelling, or contained sufficient variables for the algorithm to have learnt properly and so on.[5]

   All of the foregoing difficulties would be even more acute for a plaintiff owing to their having lower levels of resources than a regulator and greater difficulties in gaining access to proprietary software source code, input datasets and so on. During the discovery process, it is also very easy for the autonomous vehicle developer to provide incomplete access to programming source code without detection because of the volume and nature of computer software.

5.3.   DYNAMIC AND NOT STATIC STATES

One aspect of machine learning algorithms that has been hailed as one of the most powerful competencies is the ability of algorithms to improve on themselves and to obtain better results, especially in reinforcement learning

---

[1]   Jesse Levinson et al, 'Towards fully autonomous driving: Systems and algorithms', *Intelligent Vehicles Symposium (IV), 2011 IEEE* (5 July 2011) <https://www.cs.cmu.edu/~zkolter/pubs/levinson-iv2011.pdf> accessed 13 May 2018.

[2]   See Chapter 4, Section 4.2.2.

[3]   See Chapter 4, Section 4.3.4.1.

[4]   See Chapter 4, Section 4.3.4.2.

[5]   See Chapter 4, Section 4.3.4.2.

algorithms.[6] This, however, proves to be another complication for a regulator. Even if a regulator is able to have access to all of the software and input training datasets prior to the testing or deployment of an autonomous vehicle, the dynamic and not static nature of some of the machine algorithms in use may render whatever oversight or checking took place prior to the testing or deployment of an autonomous vehicle somewhat futile. The machine learning algorithm may change the mathematical and statistical models for better or for worse after the regulator has checked them. The live training datasets continuously received by the autonomous vehicle as it is tested or driven will continue to affect the algorithms and the performance of the algorithms.

Depending on how the algorithm has been constructed, it is possible for the autonomous vehicle manufacturer to 'freeze' the algorithm, so that it is no longer dynamic. However, this may create other problems depending on how the algorithms have been designed. For example, as an autonomous vehicle drives, it will collect information about its surroundings and create HD maps. If there are construction works, or the roads have changed, or a new intersection or a new roundabout has been constructed, these will be incorporated into the reference HD maps if enough autonomous vehicles sense such changes. If the autonomous vehicle has 'frozen' the algorithms, depending on the design of the algorithms, these road condition changes may not be captured or incorporated by the autonomous vehicle and this will affect its ability to drive safely through a new roundabout.

The dynamic nature of algorithms would make it rather redundant for a regulator to check machine learning algorithms before autonomous vehicles are tested or deployed on public roads.

5.4.   COMPUTER AND CYBERSECURITY AND CYBER TERRORISM

From the perspective of the regulator, it also needs to concern itself with problems of computer and cybersecurity breaches as well as terrorism because such breaches affect how the autonomous vehicle operates. Autonomous vehicles can be hacked into and controlled by terrorists to commit terrorist acts. The damage can be particularly severe if the autonomous vehicle is a heavy vehicle such as a truck. There would not be any need for terrorists to commit suicide whilst carrying out their attacks and it would be virtually impossible for law enforcement officials to capture the perpetrators as the terrorists, controlling the autonomous vehicle remotely, would only need to ram the autonomous

---

6   Stuart Russell and Peter Novig, *Artificial Intelligence: A Modern Approach* (3rd edn, Pearson 2010), ch 21.

vehicle into large obstacles to create a huge explosion and fire, which would destroy all on-board evidence.

The use of End User Agreements such as those that contract out of liability with the end user, typically used by desktop computer system software developers, especially for operating systems and office suites such as word processors, has misled many into the perception that it is not possible to have bug-free computer software programs. This is not true, and in fact, when this author was studying computer science in the 1980s, it was impressed upon all computer science students that computer programs had to be bug-free. Indeed, many people would not deposit their hard-earned savings with banks if banks were to contract out of liability with their customers in the event that moneys deposited with the banks go missing as a result of a computer security breach. There is no reason why the safety of human beings should be treated or regulated at a lesser level than moneys deposited in bank accounts.

To be clear, not only is it possible and necessary for the software on autonomous vehicles to be free from bugs and other security issues, but manufacturers of autonomous vehicles should not be allowed to contract out of liability in the event that software contains bugs or security issues.

5.4.1.   Tesla Model S Security Breaches

There have been numerous reported incidences where security loopholes have been discovered on autonomous vehicles. In September 2016, a few months after Joshua Brown was killed in his Tesla Model S crash in the US, security researchers at a software security company in China demonstrated in an 8 minute video clip the various ways they were able to gain remote access to the Tesla Model S.[7] They gained access to the Tesla's controller area network (CAN Bus) and demonstrated the various ways that the security flaws could be exploited by those wanting to do harm.

In the video clip,[8] the researchers showed that they were able to remotely control the infotainment screen, open and close the sunroof, turn on and off the signalling lights, adjust the driver's seat and unlock a locked Tesla car. Further, whilst the Tesla was in motion and driving, the researchers also demonstrated that they could remotely activate the windshield wipers, fold the side mirrors, open the boot (or the fifth door, as the Tesla Model S was a hatchback design) and even apply the brakes from 12 miles away.

---

[7]   Jay Ramey, 'Chinese hackers control Tesla brakes, lights from 12 miles away', *Autoweek* (21 September 2016) <http://autoweek.com/article/technology/tesla-patches -security-flaw-after-hackers-china-gain-access-model-s> accessed 13 May 2018.

[8]   Video clip is available at ibid.

The security company advised that it was working with Tesla to rectify the security problems and advised Tesla vehicle owners to download and update the vehicle's software.[9] Tesla tried to play down the security flaw and stated that the breach was only possible when the vehicle's web browser was used, and also required the vehicle to be physically near and connected to a malicious Wi-Fi hotspot.[10] Nevertheless, the researchers believe that the method they used can work on all vehicles that feature a web browser as part of the infotainment system.[11]

5.4.2.   Jeep Cherokee, GM, Chrysler, BMW and Mercedes Security Breaches

The Jeep Cherokee (Jeep) is not an autonomous vehicle but the fact that it is a conventional vehicle and also had severe software security vulnerabilities shows that the problem is even more acute for autonomous vehicles. Autonomous vehicles need to be constantly connected to the outside world to be able to drive, such as constantly receiving and sending GPS coordinates and receiving information about the surrounding environment, but it is these connections that open up exploits for hackers to manipulate.

In 2015, a journalist agreed to be the crash dummy for two computer security researchers and the experiment was recorded via a video.[12] The researchers, Miller and Valasek, who were located many miles away, were able to turn on the Jeep's air conditioning system, change the radio station and turn the volume to full blast, and activate the windshield wipers and windscreen fluids while the Jeep was in full motion. Not only were the researchers able to control these systems, but there was nothing that the journalist who was driving the Jeep could do inside the Jeep to stop or reverse any of their actions.

To highlight how deadly the software security flaw can be, the researchers decided to disable the transmission whilst the Jeep was on the highway. No matter how hard the journalist depressed the accelerator, the Jeep would not move. The journalist reported a near collision with a truck. Other functions on the Jeep that the researchers were able to control included the brakes, abruptly engaging them or disabling them altogether. They were also able to hijack

---

[9]   Ibid.
[10]   Ibid.
[11]   Ibid.
[12]   Unless otherwise stated, the rest of this section is taken from Andy Greenberg, 'Hackers remotely kill a Jeep on the highway – With me in it', *Wired* (21 July 2015) <https://www.wired.com/2015/07/hackers-remotely-kill-jeep-highway/> accessed 13 May 2018.

the steering wheel when the Jeep was in reverse and to track the Jeep's GPS coordinates, measuring its speed.

It appears that the vulnerability lay in the Jeep's Uconnect, an Internet-connected computer feature that controls the vehicle's entertainment and navigation, enables phone calls and even offers a Wi-Fi hot spot. The Uconnect's cellular connection also lets anyone who knows the Jeep's IP address gain access from anywhere in the country. From this access, the researchers were able to rewrite the chip's firmware, which could then send commands through the Jeep's CAN bus to its physical components, such as the engine and brake system.

Indeed, it appears that practically any modern vehicle could be vulnerable to being hacked[13] according to University of California San Diego computer science Professor Stefan Savage, who himself was involved in research in 2011 that remotely disabled the locks and brakes on a saloon car. Security experts have also been able to hack into other vehicles from other manufacturers, including GM, Chrysler, BMW and Mercedes.[14]

5.5.   STRICT LIABILITY ON AUTONOMOUS VEHICLES' SOFTWARE

Automakers need to be held accountable for their vehicles' digital security. Consumers need to realize that this is an issue, as do regulators. These kinds of software bugs are ones that can kill innocent victims.

With the various terrorism acts occurring in recent years involving vehicles in Berlin, London, Paris, Barcelona, Stockholm, Nice and elsewhere,[15] regulators should be cognizant of the real possibility of autonomous vehicles being hacked into and then used as weapons to commit terrorist acts.

Given the difficulties and challenges already highlighted regarding regulators themselves checking the software of autonomous vehicles before testing or deployment, and given the serious and real dangers of autonomous vehicles being hacked into to commit mass violence such as terrorism, not to mention their algorithms not performing reliably on a day-to-day basis, it is

---

[13]   See also Federal Bureau of Investigation, 'Motor vehicles increasingly vulnerable to remote exploits', *Public Service Announcement Alert Number I-031716-PSA* (17 March 2016) <https://www.ic3.gov/media/2016/160317.aspx> accessed 13 May 2018.

[14]   Andy Greenberg, 'Your BMW or Benz could also be vulnerable to that GM Onstar hack', *Wired* (13 August 2015) <https://www.wired.com/2015/08/bmw-benz-also-vulnerable-gm-onstar-hack/> accessed 13 May 2018.

[15]   'Timeline of vehicle rampage attacks in Europe', *The Telegraph* (9 April 2018) https://www.telegraph.co.uk/cars/news/timeline-vehicle-terror-attacks-europe/ accessed 13 May 2018.

simply nearly *impossible* for a regulator to take a micro-regulatory approach of checking each manufacturers' autonomous vehicles. In addition, there is the dynamic nature of machine learning algorithms on autonomous vehicles to contend with. All of this leads to the conclusion that the best course of action for regulators would be to mandate a system of strict liability for autonomous vehicles when they are in autonomous mode or when they have been hacked, whether in the testing stage or when they are deployed.

Strict liability is the only way to ensure public safety. It will curb any misleading or deceptive conduct by autonomous vehicle manufacturers and will also engender a responsible culture in the development of autonomous vehicles, and not one driven by profits and kudos. Whilst it may undoubtedly slow down innovation in this area, enough lives have already been lost in this area that not imposing strict liability is not justifiable given the technical constraints faced by regulators and other parties such as potential plaintiffs. The manufacturers and developers of autonomous vehicles are the only ones who know intimately how their autonomous vehicles have been constructed, hence they are in the best position to bear the financial and other risks.

Strict liability will also ensure trust in autonomous vehicles as the general public will have recourse to compensation when things go amiss. Trust further ensures the viable acceptance and take-up of autonomous vehicles. Trust is a highly valuable ethical principle, as will be discussed in Chapter 6. Ultimately, there will be much reliance on insurance law and insurance schemes as the industry of autonomous vehicles matures.[16]

One commentator has also argued for strict liability for autonomous vehicles using an analogy from the strict liability framework of early aviation.[17] This line of reasoning draws from the American Law Institute Restatement, which adopts the 'approach that if a new, unique, and relatively unexplored industry causes damage or injury, then that particular industry is subject to strict liability'.[18] It is understandable why strict liability ought to be imposed on new or novel products and technologies – they simply have not been tested openly and sufficiently for the general public to trust them and for the general public to bear the risk of their presence and use. Thus, the manufacturer must be willing and ready to stand fully by their products.

Strict liability is not a new concept in many jurisdictions, although it is one that may only be applicable in limited settings owing to the possibility that it

---

[16] See Chapter 6, Section 6.21.

[17] Adam Rosenberg, 'Strict liability: Imagining a legal framework for autonomous vehicles' (2017) 20 Tulane Journal of Technology and Intellectual Property 205. See also Gary E Marchant and Rachel A Lindor, 'The coming collision between autonomous vehicles and the liability system' (2012) 52 Santa Clara Law Review 1321.

[18] Ibid, 219.

may be too harsh. Strict liability has nevertheless been imposed on the manufacturer of products for defects in many jurisdictions.

5.5.1. Strict Liability in the US for Product Defects

The current product liability laws in the US generally suggest strict liability for product defects. Indeed, a number of commentators have rightly pointed to the tests in law for establishing product defects and the imposition of strict liability for product defects, and have argued for their application to manufacturers of autonomous vehicles. However, these commentators do not seem to realize that the existing tests in the current laws will be very difficult, if not impossible, to apply owing to the nature and complexities of machine learning algorithms.[19]

Courts in the US have generally used two tests to determine whether a product has a design defect; the first is the objective consumer test and the second is the risk-utility test.[20] Regarding the first test, the Restatement (Second) of Torts provides that a product is defective if it is 'dangerous to an extent beyond that which would be contemplated by the ordinary consumer who purchases it'.[21] The use of the objective ordinary consumer is not an issue in this formulation, but to determine when something is 'dangerous to an extent beyond' what the reasonable consumer would expect from a product could be an issue as it may not be possible to determine the question of 'extent'. If an autonomous vehicle can navigate one roundabout without problems but crashes at the next roundabout, and the plaintiff cannot access, or cannot comprehend the machine learning algorithms on the entire autonomous vehicle, how does one determine the question of 'extent'?

As for the second test, Restatement (Third) of Torts states that:[22]

> [T]he foreseeable risks of harm posed by the product could have been reduced or avoided by the adoption of a reasonable alternative design by the seller or other dis-

---

[19] See for example Jeffrey K Gurney, 'Crashing into the unknown: An examination of crash-optimization algorithms through the two lanes of ethics and law' (2015–2016) 79 Albany Law Review 183; Matthew Blunt, 'Highway to a headache: Is tort-based automotive insurance on a collision course with autonomous vehicles' (2017) 53 Willamette Law Review 107; Bryant Walker Smith, 'Automated driving and product liability' [2017] Michigan State Law Review 1; Melinda Florina Lohmann, 'Liability issues concerning self-driving vehicles' (2016) 7 European Journal of Risk Regulation 335; Gary E Marchant and Rachel A Lindor (n 17).

[20] David G Owen, 'Design defects' (2008) 73 Missouri Law Review 291, 299.

[21] Restatement (Second) of Torts § 402A cmt i (Am. Law Inst. 1965).

[22] Restatement (Third) of Torts: Product Liability § 2(b) (Am. Law Inst. 1998).

tributor, or a predecessor in the commercial chain of distribution, and the omission of the alternative design renders the product not reasonably safe.

Again, this test is very difficult to apply to machine learning algorithms as it enquires about an alternative design. At the best of times, it will be extremely difficult to discern the design of any given algorithm as it will be, for example, impossible to check through all of the training datasets fed to the algorithms, let alone suggest an alternative design.

While the current laws in the US appear to suggest that manufacturers of autonomous vehicles will bear the liability where there are defects, this is not necessarily easy to establish in the technical sense.

5.5.2.   Strict Liability in the EU for Product Defects

In Europe, the legislation may appear less acutely problematic but there are nevertheless still challenges. The EU Directive 85/374/EEC on product liability[23] stipulates a regime of strict liability to member states of the EU. Article 1 of the EU Directive states that the manufacturer shall be liable for damage caused by a defect in the product it produces.

Article 6 states:

1.   A product is defective when it does not provide the safety which a person
     is entitled to expect, taking all circumstances into account, including:
     a.   the presentation of the product;
     b.   the use to which it could reasonably be expected that the product would
          be put;
     c.   the time when the product was put into circulation.

This objective test of what a person would be entitled to expect with respect to safety is a fairly general test and would appear to set the bar quite high for manufacturers of autonomous vehicles to ensure that their vehicles are safe, do not contain programming bugs or security flaws and so on. This would be the safety level a person is entitled to expect from an autonomous vehicle and a competent driver in the driving task, and since many competent drivers never encounter accidents, the autonomous vehicle should also not encounter accidents. This view is also held by a report from a commissioned project, which concluded in 2014 with a set of *Guidelines on Regulating Robotics* (Guidelines) containing regulatory suggestions for the European

---

[23]   EU Council Directive 85/374/EEC of 25 July 1985 on the approximation of the laws, regulations and administrative provisions of the Member States concerning liability for defective products.

Commission.[24] However, the Guidelines also held the view that: 'A producer can, for example, escape product liability if he shows that the state of scientific and technical knowledge at the time when he put the product into circulation was not unable [*sic*] to detect the defect'.[25] What the authors of the Guidelines probably meant was that, if a producer can show that the state of scientific and technical knowledge at the time when the product was put into circulation was not able to detect the defect, then it can escape product liability.

Indeed, the German *Product Liability Act* specifies that, if damage to life, body or property is caused by a defect of a vehicle, the vehicle manufacturer is liable irrespective of fault, with the exception that if the defect could not have been detected based on the state of science and technology at the time when the product was put on the market. Germany implemented the EU Directive 85/374/EEC on product liability by passing a special law, the Produkthaftungsgesetz, which came into force on 1 January 1990, and it mirrors the EU Directive 85/374/EEC very closely, copying it verbatim in some parts, and adding or shortening passages in others.

Further, when Germany enacted new legislation in June 2017 allowing automated driving systems, it was heavily criticized for not including a specific product liability claim against the manufacturer of the automated vehicle but the German government's stance was that the general product liability rules should be sufficient.[26]

This kind of non-detection exception or qualification based on the state of science and technology at the time when the product was put on the market would unfortunately swing the pendulum too far in favour of the manufacturers of autonomous vehicles. This kind of argument may work well and find common sense in most arenas, especially developed ones, but it is simply meaningless in the field of machine learning algorithms. It opens the door for manufacturers of autonomous vehicles to simply assert that they were not able to check through the millions of training datasets they had fed their algorithms, and hence the scientific and technical knowledge at the time could not have detected the defect.

This line of reasoning is also circular when applied to an emerging field such as machine learning algorithms. It is primarily because the technology

[24] Erica Palmerini et al, *Guidelines on Regulating Robotics* (2014) <http://www .robolaw.eu/index.htm> accessed 13 May 2018, 58–60. See also Melinda Florina Lohmann (n 19).

[25] Erica Palmerini et al (n 24), 58.

[26] Jochen Ellrott, Rolf Trittmann and Christoph Werkmeister, 'Automated driving law passed in Germany' (21 June 2017) <https://www.freshfields.com/en-us/our -thinking/campaigns/digital/internet-of-things/connected-cars/automated-driving-law -passed-in-germany/> accessed 13 May 2018.

is immature and unsafe and full of unknowns that strict liability needs to be imposed if it is unleashed on the general public. To be able to circumvent strict liability by a qualification that feeds on the incomplete knowledge of an immature technology defeats the purpose of protecting the general public from untested technology.

5.6. MANDATING MINIMUM TECHNICAL STANDARDS

In addition to imposing strict liability, regulators should also mandate that autonomous vehicles must be equipped with the minimum devices and sensor suites, as already discussed in Chapter 3.

Other regulatory measures could include requiring the use of encryption and segmentation and layering techniques, which will separate internal systems where possible, so that a security breach of one system does not lead to a breach of the entire system.[27] These are general methodologies that would go some way towards preventing autonomous vehicles from being hacked, while allowing the autonomous vehicle developer to choose how they are to be implemented. Indeed, perhaps guidelines such as the National Highway Traffic Safety Administration (NHTSA) cybersecurity best practices should be made mandatory to help isolate and contain vulnerabilities and to dissuade hackers.[28] Similarly, NHTSA's *Automated Driving Systems, A Vision for Safety 2.0*, which outlines best practices on the safe release of autonomous vehicle technologies, could be made mandatory for autonomous vehicle manufacturers to follow.[29]

In June 2017, an amendment to the German Road Traffic Act came into effect. The amendment does not sanction trusting software to run a vehicle without human supervision, that is, autonomous driving, but it does permit automated driving systems where the driver is obliged to remain aware of the traffic and the vehicle to a degree that he or she can react in case of a malfunction or any other situation which cannot be handled by the automated driving

---

[27] National Highway Traffic Safety Administration, *Cybersecurity Best Practices for Modern Vehicles* (October 2016) (Report No. DOT HS 812 333) <https://www.nhtsa .gov/sites/nhtsa.dot.gov/files/documents/812333_cybersecurityformodernvehicles .pdf> accessed 13 May 2018.

[28] Ibid.

[29] NHTSA, *Automated Driving Systems, A Vision for Safety 2.0* (12 September 2017) <https://www.nhtsa.gov/manufacturers/automated-driving-systems> accessed 13 May 2018.

function.[30] In any event, driving a vehicle without human supervision is also not yet permitted under the Vienna Convention on Road Traffic.[31]

Included in the amendments is a requirement for all vehicles with automated driving systems must be equipped with a black box to help allocate fault and liability in the event of an accident.[32] The black box must record whether the driver or the system was in control of the vehicle, whether the system prompted the driver to take back control and whether any technical malfunctions occur.[33] The black box must also record the location where and when these events happen.[34] The black box is essentially an aid in determining liability in the event of an accident because in Germany (and many parts of Europe),[35] even if the driver is free of liability owing to the data recorded by the black box, the vehicle's owner will always be held liable vis-à-vis the accident victims under the normal and strict German car owner liability regime.[36]

Regardless of whatever liability standards are adopted, mandating that important incident data is recorded and kept must be one of the minimum requirements that regulators adopt.

5.7.   PERMISSIVE APPROACHES

This section will examine two permissive approaches to the testing and deployment of autonomous vehicles on public roads and evaluate them, taking one example from the US and one from the EU.

5.7.1.   Arizona, US

Some of the states in the US have passed legislation in recent years permitting autonomous vehicles on their roads, especially for testing purposes.[37] The US National Conference of State Legislatures has compiled a comprehensive website and has made available a new autonomous vehicles legislative database, which provides up-to-date, real-time information about state auton-

---

[30]   Jochen Ellrott, Rolf Trittmann and Christoph Werkmeister (n 26).
[31]   UN Convention on Road Traffic (Vienna, 8 November 1968) <https://treaties.un.org/pages/ViewDetailsIII.aspx?src=TREATY&mtdsg_no=XI-B-19&chapter=11&Temp=mtdsg3&clang=_en> accessed 13 May 2018.
[32]   Jochen Ellrott, Rolf Trittmann and Christoph Werkmeister (n 26).
[33]   Ibid.
[34]   Ibid.
[35]   Melinda Florina Lohmann (n 19).
[36]   Jochen Ellrott, Rolf Trittmann and Christoph Werkmeister (n 26).
[37]   See James M Anderson et al, *Autonomous Vehicle Technology: A Guide for Policymakers* (Rand Corp 2016), ch 3 for a comprehensive overview of the legislative activity.

omous vehicle legislation that has been introduced in the 50 states and the District of Columbia.[38] Nevada was the first state to authorize the operation of autonomous vehicles in 2011. Since then, 21 other states – Alabama, Arkansas, California, Colorado, Connecticut, Florida, Georgia, Illinois, Indiana, Louisiana, Michigan, New York, North Carolina, North Dakota, Pennsylvania, South Carolina, Tennessee, Texas, Utah, Virginia and Vermont – and Washington, DC have passed legislation related to autonomous vehicles. Governors in Arizona, Delaware, Hawaii, Idaho, Maine, Massachusetts, Minnesota, Ohio, Washington and Wisconsin have issued executive orders related to autonomous vehicles.[39]

From this cursory summary, it is evident that autonomous vehicles and autonomous vehicle testing is prevalent in the US. From the summary of each piece of legislation from each of the US states on the website of the National Conference of State Legislatures as at late March 2018, in most of the states but not all,[40] the legislation is permissive with perhaps some additional requirements such as requiring the autonomous vehicles meet federal standards and regulations for motor vehicles and comply with applicable traffic and motor vehicle laws of the state.[41] These standards and regulations are, by and large, quite general and are applicable to non-autonomous vehicles as well and they address the likes of ensuring that there are safety seat belts, air bags and so on.[42]

Beyond these, there appears to be no state oversight or testing of the actual functionalities of the autonomous vehicles before they are allowed on the roads. Some states do specify limitations such as geographical limits of the autonomous vehicle testing and insurance requirements, but these appear to mitigate damage rather than seriously assess the functionalities and roadworthiness of the autonomous vehicle, even in testing mode.

In Arizona, the situation seems the most permissive than any other state, with its Governor Doug Ducey signing an executive order in late August 2015 directing various agencies to 'undertake any necessary steps to support

---

[38] National Conference of State Legislatures, 'Autonomous vehicles/self-driving vehicles enacted legislation' <http://www.ncsl.org/research/transportation/autonomous -vehicles-self-driving-vehicles-enacted-legislation.aspx> accessed 27 May 2018.

[39] Ibid.

[40] Ibid. One notable exception is New York, which requires direct supervision of New York state police for the testing of autonomous vehicles.

[41] Ibid.

[42] Motor Vehicle Safety 2013, Title 49, United States Code, Chapter 301 and Related Uncodified Provisions administered by the National Highway Traffic Safety Administration (May 2013) <https://www.nhtsa.gov/sites/nhtsa.dot.gov/files/ documents/motor_vehicle_safety_unrelated_uncodified_provisions_may2013.pdf> accessed 27 May 2018.

the testing and operation of self-driving vehicles on public roads within Arizona'.[43] On 1 March 2018, Governor Ducey updated the 2015 executive order with Executive Order 2018-04.[44] This updated order allows the testing of autonomous vehicles without a safety driver inside the vehicle. In terms of the requirements before testing without a person inside the autonomous vehicle is allowed, the vehicle must be fully autonomous and the operator of the test autonomous vehicles must submit a written statement to the Arizona Department of Transportation acknowledging that:[45]

a. Unless an exemption or waiver has been granted by the National Highway Traffic Safety Administration, the fully autonomous vehicle is equipped with an automated driving system that is in compliance with all applicable federal law and federal motor vehicle safety standards and bears the required certification label(s) including reference to any exemption granted under applicable federal law;

b. If a failure of the automated driving system occurs that renders that system unable to perform the entire dynamic driving task relevant to its intended operational design domain, the fully autonomous vehicle will achieve a minimal risk condition;

c. The fully autonomous vehicle is capable of complying with all applicable traffic and motor vehicle safety laws and regulations of the State of Arizona, and the person testing or operating the fully autonomous vehicle may be issued a traffic citation or other applicable penalty in the event the vehicle fails to comply with traffic and/or motor vehicle laws; and

d. the fully autonomous vehicle meets all applicable certificate, title registration, licensing and insurance requirements.

It appears that Arizona has adopted a self-certification system with the operator who wishes to test autonomous vehicles to simply provide a written statement that the 'fully autonomous vehicle is capable of complying with all applicable traffic and motor vehicle safety laws and regulations of the State of Arizona'.[46]

Further, the only safety requirement imposed is that if the autonomous vehicle is not able to perform the 'entire dynamic driving task', it 'will achieve a minimal risk condition' without even specifying what the minimal risk condition might be.[47] For some autonomous vehicle developers, this may well mean to continue driving, perhaps back to headquarters.

---

43 Ibid.
44 State of Arizona Executive Order, Order 2018-04 <https://azgovernor.gov/sites/default/files/related-docs/eo2018-04_1.pdf> accessed 27 May 2018.
45 State of Arizona Executive Order, Order 2018-04 (n 44) paragraph 3.
46 State of Arizona Executive Order, Order 2018-04 (n 44) paragraph 3(c).
47 State of Arizona Executive Order, Order 2018-04 (n 44) paragraph 3(b).

As for paragraphs 3(a) and 3(d), these are not specific to autonomous vehicles and are applicable to non-autonomous vehicles as well, hence they do not address the novel and new safety issues raised by autonomous vehicles.

There is no mention of how liability should be apportioned in the Executive Order, which means that it defaults to current laws, making it extremely difficult for victims to be successful in legal actions in negligence or under product liability laws.

By adopting a self-certification system without specifying strict liability for the manufacturers of autonomous vehicles, the state of Arizona is in effect abdicating its duty to govern and to protect the citizens within its state. Autonomous vehicles operate through sensors and largely a bunch of mathematical and statistical algorithms which have not yet been thoroughly tested. The technology is not even at the state of maturity, let alone be permitted to be unleashed onto public roads and the general unsuspecting public, without any special and specific legal protections given to the general public. It has been reported that Arizona has been aggressively courting autonomous vehicle researchers, even embarking on Twitter campaigns aimed at wooing companies from Silicon Valley.[48] It appears to have a singular pursuit to win the race amongst the states in autonomous vehicles without much regard to the safety of human lives. It is perhaps not a coincidence that the first pedestrian fatality in the US involving an autonomous vehicle occurred in Arizona within weeks of the signing of the Executive Order by Governor Ducey when Uber's autonomous vehicle[49] killed Elaine Herzberg.

5.7.2. Germany

When Germany amended its Road Traffic Act in mid 2017, it did so cautiously and attempted to provide some safeguards. The legislative changes allowed automated driving systems but not autonomous driving and the driver must be ready to immediately take over the driving at all times.[50] It further provides

---

48   Alex Hern, 'Google's Waymo invites members of public to trial self-driving vehicles', *The Guardian* (27 April 2017) <https://www.theguardian.com/technology/2017/apr/25/google-self-driving-waymo-invites-members-public-trial-vehicles-phoenix-arizona> accessed 27 May 2018.

49   Nathan Bomey, 'Uber self-driving car crash: Vehicle detected Arizona pedestrian 6 seconds before accident', *USA Today* (24 May 2018) <https://www.usatoday.com/story/money/cars/2018/05/24/uber-self-driving-car-crash-ntsb-investigation/640123002/> accessed 27 May 2018.

50   German Road Traffic Act; *Straßenverkehrsgesetz* § 1b <https://www.gesetze-im-internet.de/stvg/__1b.html> accessed 27 May 2018.

that the driver must use the automated driving function as intended,[51] for example, if it is only intended for use on highways, it should not be used within townships.

Like Arizona, the German law adopts a self-certification system, which requires the vehicle manufacturer to confirm[52] that the vehicle is equipped with a highly or fully automated driving system that is able to:[53]

1. control the driving task after being activated;
2. comply with the traffic regulations in line with the driving situation;
3. be manually overridden and deactivated by the driver at any time;
4. recognize situations when the driver must take manual control;
5. notify the driver sufficiently in advance of such situations where the driver must take manual control by means of optical, acoustic, tactile or other warning; and
6. indicate that there is a use that is contrary to the description of the system.

German law permits the driver to avert his/her attention from the traffic and the vehicle control when the vehicle is controlled by the highly or fully automated driving functions but the driver must remain sufficiently aware and responsive in order to immediately regain control of the vehicle when prompted by the system or when the driver realizes that the preconditions for the automated driving mode are no longer fulfilled (for example, if the automated system on the vehicle is intended for highway driving but the vehicle is exiting a highway).[54]

It appears that the German lawmakers have ignored well-established research highlighted in Chapter 3[55] that has shown that humans are not capable of monitoring an automated system and are likely to become bored and disengaged,[56] fallible, distractable and, perhaps, easily seduced by machines that appear to function safely.[57] As such, it is improbable that humans will be able

---

[51]   German Road Traffic Act; *Straßenverkehrsgesetz* § 1a(1) <https://www.gesetze -im-internet.de/stvg/1a.html> accessed 27 May 2018.
[52]   German Road Traffic Act; *Straßenverkehrsgesetz* § 1a(2) <https://www.gesetze -im-internet.de/stvg/__1a.html> accessed 27 May 2018.
[53]   Ibid.
[54]   German Road Traffic Act; *Straßenverkehrsgesetz* § 1b <https://www.gesetze-im -internet.de/stvg/__1b.html> accessed 27 May 2018.
[55]   See Sections 3.3.1 and 3.7.6.
[56]   Sam Levin, 'Uber crash shows "catastrophic failure" of self-driving tech-nology, experts say', *The Guardian* (22 March 2018) <https://www.theguardian .com/technology/2018/mar/22/self-driving-car-uber-death-woman-failure-fatal-crash -arizona> accessed 13 May 2018.
[57]   Olivia Solon, 'Who's driving? Autonomous cars may be entering the most dangerous phase', *The Guardian* (24 January 2018) <https://www.theguardian.com/

to physically regain control of the vehicle immediately as required by the law. It is also unclear how long drivers are allowed to avert their attention away from traffic. Given that driving on Germany's Autobahns attracts an advisory speed limit of 130 kilometres an hour, even 1 second of inattention could prove deadly.

It would also appear that this provision is contrary to ethical guidelines in Germany, which mandate that humans must not be required to take over control of a vehicle 'abruptly'. This is further discussed in Chapter 6.[58]

Lastly, this provision allowing attention to be turned away from traffic and vehicle control has an underlying assumption that the autonomous vehicle is developed and sophisticated and that the autonomous system is capable of driving itself in a highly functional way. This underlying assumption is not true at this present time as the current stage of autonomous vehicle development has not reached maturity, hence this provision really should not be applicable when autonomous vehicles are still at the developmental testing stage. It appears the German legislature is courting disaster with this provision.

It is unclear what the legal significance of the manufacturer's declaration of compliance with the list of six items defining a highly or fully automated driving system is. The declaration in item 2, that it will comply with the traffic regulations in line with the driving situation, may be of significance in questions of liability. If this declaration can be held binding against the manufacturer with respect to the world at large, especially with respect to accident victims, it could be a useful weapon either independently as a warranty or in combination with existing European and German product liability laws for defects.[59] There may be room to argue that if a manufacturer confirms through the declaration that its vehicle is able to comply with the traffic regulations in line with the driving situation, then this is the absolute safety level that the general public would expect for the product and any deviation from this would be a clear product defect, triggering strict liability. Using this line of argument, it leaves no room for any consideration of whether the defect could have been detected given the state of science and technology at the time when the product was put on the market.

From the foregoing, it is evident that the German permissive approach to the regulation of semi-autonomous and autonomous vehicles is a far more responsible, cautious and satisfactory approach than the approach of Arizona. The German approach would impose strict liability should a vehicle not be able

---

technology/2018/jan/24/self-driving-cars-dangerous-period-false-security> accessed 23 April 2018.

[58]   See Chapter 6, Section 6.17.

[59]   See above, Section 5.5.2.

to safely navigate new intersections and roundabouts, road constructions and so on. However, the German regulatory approach may not adequately address the situation where there is a cybersecurity breach. For example, if a security breach occurs that does not breach traffic regulations, but instead takes the vehicle to a different destination, as in the case of a kidnapping or carjacking, then the victim may have to fall back on the general product defects law, which will undoubtedly trigger considerations of whether the security breach was one that could have been detected given the state of science and technology.

In addition to the possibility of the imposition of strict liability on manufacturers of autonomous vehicles, the German approach also gives due consideration to data protection, a topic which is beyond the scope of this work.

Lastly, the German amendments were introduced together with a set of ethical guidelines for autonomous vehicles. This will be considered in Chapter 6.

6. Ethical responsibilities and autonomous vehicles

The question of ethics in the programming of autonomous vehicles has received substantial attention in recent years with many scholars theorizing on the issue.[1] The aim of this chapter, however, is not to review the current academic discourse, partly because the ethical questions have too often been too narrowly framed by scholars. Instead, it will turn its attention to a set of ethical guidelines, which are broader and more practically useful at this present point in time.

To be clear, questions concerning whether an autonomous vehicle should stop at a pedestrian crossing are not ethical issues – these are legal issues as they have already been covered by or stipulated in traffic laws and regulations. Similarly, whether the vehicle should swerve and/or apply the brakes to avoid colliding with a child who suddenly runs onto the road is also technically not an ethics question because such a situation is already covered under traffic laws requiring drivers to maintain a proper lookout, which would require the vehicle to swerve and/or apply the brakes. So, what would be an ethics question?

Many scholars begin by focussing on what is termed the 'trolley problem'. Philippa Foot ignited decades of thought and debate when she introduced the problems of two scenarios, which later evolved to be called the transplant case and the trolley problem.[2] Foot, being British, originally wrote the trolley

---

[1]   See for example Jeffrey K Gurney, 'Crashing into the unknown: An examination of crash-optimization algorithms through the two lanes of ethics and law' (2015–2016) 79 Albany Law Review 183; Jason Millar, 'An ethics evaluation tool for automating ethical decision-making in robots and self-driving cars' (2016) 30 Applied Artificial Intelligence 787; Catherine Nunez, 'Artificial intelligence and legal ethics: Whether AI lawyers can make ethical decisions' (2017) 20 Tulane Journal of Technology and Intellectual Property 189; Sven Nyholm and Jilles Smids, 'The ethics of accident-algorithms for self-driving cars: An applied trolley problem?' (2016) 19 Ethical Theory and Moral Practice 1275; Santoni de Sio, 'Killing by autonomous vehicles and the legal doctrine of necessity' (2017) 20 Ethical Theory and Moral Practice 1275; Pawel Zgrzebnicki, 'Selected ethical issues in artificial intelligence, autonomous system development and large data set processing' (2017) 6 Studia Humana 24.

[2]   Philippa Foot, 'The problem of abortion and the doctrine of double effect' in *Virtues and Vices: And Other Essays in Moral Philosophy* (2002 OUP), 24–25. The essay was originally published in 1967 in *Oxford Review*.

problem as a tram driver problem,[3] but since trams are better known in North America as trolleys, the language of the trolley problem has endured as philosophers from across the Atlantic have taken up the debate.

In the tram driver problem, the driver of a runaway tram finds himself only able to steer from one narrow track onto another; five men are working on one track and one man on the other. Anyone on the track he enters is bound to be killed, there is no possibility of escape or hanging to side ladders in the tram tunnel or any other alternative. Would it be morally permissible for the driver to steer to the less occupied track or, as some would suggest, must the driver steer to the less occupied track? Under consequentialism, steering to the less occupied track would not only be permissible but some consequentialists might even argue that the driver must do this.[4] Foot, however, exposed the problems with such an approach.[5] Thus begins the debate of ethics and autonomous vehicles. Ethicists and lawyers have used this tram/trolley problem as a springboard for discussions on the ethical issues of computer programming, such as whether computer programs should be written in such a way so as to kill one, instead of killing five.[6]

It is not the aim of this chapter to delve into such discourse. Indeed, as the preceding chapters have shown,[7] this kind of question may be moot in non-hard-coded software such as machine learning algorithms, as the software programmer is not writing any software to hard code into the program whether one person or five people should be killed. The use of training datasets in machine learning algorithms can, of course, affect what kinds of decisions the algorithm makes, but the algorithms and the complexities thereof are still in their infancy in the field of autonomous vehicles. This is not to say that such issues are unimportant. They are indeed critical issues, but for the purposes of this chapter, they are too narrowly focused on the programming task. The question of ethics in the whole development and regulation of autonomous vehicles must take a broader view at the present point in time.

For this reason, this chapter will focus on the first guidelines in the world for autonomous vehicles, dated June 2017 and presented by the Ethics Commission on Automated Driving set up by the German Ministry of Transport and Digital

---

[3]   Ibid, 23–24.
[4]   Judith Jarvis Thomson, 'The Trolley Problem' (1985) 94 Yale Law Journal 1395–1415 at 1395.
[5]   Philippa Foot (n 2).
[6]   See n 1.
[7]   See for example Chapter 4.

Infrastructure in August 2017.[8] The German federal government has adopted the guidelines for autonomous vehicles within Germany.

The 14 members of the Ethics Commission on Automated Driving comprised academics and experts from the disciplines of ethics, law and technology and included transport experts, legal experts, information scientists, engineers, philosophers, theologians and consumer protection representatives as well as representatives of associations and companies. The Report essentially comprises 20 guidelines, which at their core prioritize the value and equality of human life over damage to property or animals.[9] The 20 guidelines are a fairly comprehensive and mostly sound first attempt at addressing the ethical aspects of autonomous vehicles. Each one of the guidelines will now be examined and, for completeness, each guideline will be reproduced in full.

6.1.   GUIDELINE 1[10]

> The primary purpose of partly and fully automated transport systems is to improve safety for all road users. Another purpose is to increase mobility opportunities and to make further benefits possible. Technological development obeys the principle of personal autonomy, which means that individuals enjoy freedom of action for which they themselves are responsible.

To ensure that there are no doubts, Guideline 1 clearly lays down the purposes of autonomous vehicles: to improve safety for all road users and to increase mobility opportunities. There is no mention of convenience, which is what companies such as Tesla have been promoting over the years.[11] The purposes set out in Guideline 1 represent the core of what autonomous vehicles ought to be concerned with: first and foremost improving safety and secondly increasing mobility, for example, for those who may be physically challenged. Guideline 1 also sets out the principle of personal autonomy, which undoubted seeks to restore to the individual some semblance of autonomy given the seemingly overwhelming dictates of technologies.

---

[8]   German Ministry of Transport and Digital Infrastructure Press Release 084/2017, 'Ethics Commission on Automated Driving presents report' (28 August 2017) <https://www.bmvi.de/SharedDocs/EN/PressRelease/2017/084-ethic-commission-report-automated-driving.html> accessed 13 May 2018.

[9]   Ethics Commission, Federal Ministry of Transport and Digital Infrastructure, *Automated and Connected Driving Report* (June 2017) <https://www.bmvi.de/SharedDocs/EN/publications/report-ethics-commission.pdf?__blob=publicationFile> accessed 13 May 2018.

[10]   Ethics Commission (n 9), 10.

[11]   See Chapter 3.

In terms of implementing the principle of personal autonomy, autonomous vehicle developers would need to provide individuals with choices, wherever possible and legally permissible to do so. For example, drivers would not be able to choose whether to stop at a red traffic light or to accelerate, but they should be able to choose the driving speed, as long as the choice of speed is below the speed limit.

6.2.   GUIDELINE 2[12]

> The protection of individuals takes precedence over all other utilitarian considerations. The objective is to reduce the level of harm until it is completely prevented. The licensing of automated systems is not justifiable unless it promises to produce at least a diminution in harm compared with human driving, in other words a positive balance of risk.

Guideline 2 places the protection of human beings as the highest priority and advocates the minimization of harm principle. This is indeed a much needed declaration as a reminder to autonomous vehicle developers that they must not release half-baked technologies on the general public to test out as human guinea-pigs for utilitarian reasons such as profits or to win the autonomous vehicle technology race. This is, of course, in addition to the guidance to computer programmers that they must value human life and not program their software in a cavalier manner that allows human beings to be run over. A case in point here of the poor implementation of both of these is the Uber crash in Arizona that killed a pedestrian, Elaine Herzberg. The Preliminary Report from the NTSB stated that Uber's autonomous vehicle had 'classified the pedestrian as an unknown object, as a vehicle, and then as a bicycle with varying expectations of future travel path'.[13] If Uber's technology cannot firstly even correctly classify the pedestrian as a pedestrian, it is obviously immature technology and secondly, in not being able to detect the pedestrian and then killing Herzberg when the autonomous vehicle failed to stop, it is not protecting individuals.

Guideline 2 also seems to present the standpoint that, unless the use of autonomous vehicles 'promises' to decrease the harm compared with human driving, they should not be permitted on the roads. The operative word here is 'promises': the technology does not have to actually decrease harm, there just needs to be a possibility or likelihood it will. This loose standard is not stating

---

[12]   Ethics Commission (n 9), 10.
[13]   NTSB, *Preliminary Report Highway HWY18MH010* <http://www.ntsb.gov/ investigations/AccidentReports/Reports?HWY18MH010-prelim.pdf> accessed 30 May 2018, 2.

anything new and appears to be a re-statement of the current situation where there is much hype about the wonderful capabilities of autonomous vehicles.

6.3. GUIDELINE 3[14]

> The public sector is responsible for guaranteeing the safety of the automated and connected systems introduced and licensed in the public street environment. Driving systems thus need official licensing and monitoring. The guiding principle is the avoidance of accidents, although technologically unavoidable residual risks do not militate against the introduction of automated driving if the balance of risks is fundamentally positive.

Guideline 3 appears to be sending a couple of messages. The first is that the public sector, that is the government, has the responsibility for guaranteeing the safety of the general public if autonomous vehicles are introduced on public roads, and they must be licensed and monitored. This is certainly the expected role of governments and is in stark contrast to the position in Arizona.

The second message in Guideline 3 appears to be that whilst there is a need for safety, 'technologically unavoidable residual risks' appear to be acceptable. It is unclear what would classify as 'technologically unavoidable residual risks' and it will be interesting to see how this is defined.

6.4. GUIDELINE 4[15]

> The personal responsibility of individuals for taking decisions is an expression of a society centred on individual human beings, with their entitlement to personal development and their need for protection. The purpose of all governmental and political regulatory decisions is thus to promote the free development and the protection of individuals. In a free society, the way in which technology is statutorily fleshed out is such that a balance is struck between maximum personal freedom of choice in a general regime of development and the freedom of others and their safety.

Guideline 4 appears to be an extension and elaboration of Guideline 1. Personal autonomy in Guideline 1 is here extended to protection of 'personal development' and 'free society'. The underlying principle appears to be that technological development must take place within the confines of protecting an individual's freedom of choice as well as the freedom of others and their safety.

---

[14] Ethics Commission (n 9), 10.
[15] Ibid.

6.5.   GUIDELINE 5[16]

Automated and connected technology should prevent accidents wherever this is practically possible. Based on the state of the art, the technology must be designed in such a way that critical situations do not arise in the first place. These include dilemma situations, in other words a situation in which an automated vehicle has to 'decide' which of two evils, between which there can be no trade-off, it necessarily has to perform. In this context, the entire spectrum of technological options – for instance from limiting the scope of application to controllable traffic environments, vehicle sensors and braking performance, signals for persons at risk, right up to preventing hazards by means of 'intelligent' road infrastructure – should be used and continuously evolved. The significant enhancement of road safety is the objective of development and regulation, starting with the design and programming of the vehicles such that they drive in a defensive and anticipatory manner, posing as little risk as possible to vulnerable road users.

Guideline 5 articulates precisely how autonomous vehicle development ought to be designed, so that critical situations, such as the trolley problem, do not arise in the first place. It also highlights how it is possible to achieve this road utopia through methodologies such as controllable traffic environments, vehicle sensors and braking performance, signals for persons at risk and 'intelligent' road infrastructure. Chapters 3 and 4 were focused on how to achieve such vehicle-related methodologies through use of the sensor suites, devices, emergency braking systems and software on-board autonomous vehicles. There is much more that can be done to improve the traffic environment, such as road infrastructure that makes the roads make more sense to autonomous vehicles. For example, lane markings are painted white – perhaps they can be coated with a substance that is easier for autonomous vehicles to detect instead of having to rely on lidar signals matched with camera images, and so on.

6.6.   GUIDELINE 6[17]

The introduction of more highly automated driving systems, especially with the option of automated collision prevention, may be socially and ethically mandated if it can unlock existing potential for damage limitation. Conversely, a statutorily imposed obligation to use fully automated transport systems or the causation of practical inescapabilty is ethically questionable if it entails submission to technological imperatives (prohibition on degrading the subject to a mere network element).

Guideline 6 appears to be a reminder and warning that fully automated driving should not be made mandatory. Not only would making autonomous vehicles

---

[16]   Ibid.
[17]   Ibid, 11.

mandatory be contrary to personal autonomy (Guideline 1), but the concern here is that it might reduce individuals to 'a mere network element', a possible reference to the Kantian perspective, to reduce humans to mere means to an end in the technological architecture.

6.7.   GUIDELINE 7[18]

In hazardous situations that prove to be unavoidable, despite all technological precautions being taken, the protection of human life enjoys top priority in a balancing of legally protected interests. Thus, within the constraints of what is technologically feasible, the systems must be programmed to accept damage to animals or property in a conflict if this means that personal injury can be prevented.

Guideline 7 is straightforward as it simply states that the protection of human life is the foremost priority. Damage to property and also to animals is acceptable and mandated in order to prevent injury to humans or to save a human life.

6.8.   GUIDELINE 8[19]

Genuine dilemmatic decisions, such as a decision between one human life and another, depend on the actual specific situation, incorporating 'unpredictable' behaviour by parties affected. They can thus not be clearly standardized, nor can they be programmed such that they are ethically unquestionable. Technological systems must be designed to avoid accidents. However, they cannot be standardized to a complex or intuitive assessment of the impacts of an accident in such a way that they can replace or anticipate the decision of a responsible driver with the moral capacity to make correct judgements. It is true that a human driver would be acting unlawfully if he killed a person in an emergency to save the lives of one or more other persons, but he would not necessarily be acting culpably. Such legal judgements, made in retrospect and taking special circumstances into account, cannot readily be transformed into abstract/general ex ante appraisals and thus also not into corresponding programming activities. For this reason, perhaps more than any other, it would be desirable for an independent public sector agency (for instance a Federal Bureau for the Investigation of Accidents Involving Automated Transport Systems or a Federal Office for Safety in Automated and Connected Transport) to systematically process the lessons learned.

Guideline 8 sums up aptly the current state of the technology, that it is simply not possible for software to be standardized to form a complex or intuitive assessment of the impacts of an accident. Chapter 4 sought to demonstrate this fact through the workings of the types of software on autonomous vehicles and

---

[18]   Ibid.
[19]   Ibid.

everyone, including regulators, philosophers and lawyers, should be cognizant of this. Indeed, this is one of the confines within which autonomous vehicles need to operate, so the best course is for all to recognize this limitation and work around it.

6.9.   GUIDELINE 9[20]

> In the event of unavoidable accident situations, any distinction based on personal features (age, gender, physical or mental constitution) is strictly prohibited. It is also prohibited to offset victims against one another. General programming to reduce the number of personal injuries may be justifiable. Those parties involved in the generation of mobility risks must not sacrifice non-involved parties.

Guideline 9 is one of the more controversial guidelines. It begins uncontroversially by prohibiting programmers from choosing harm to individuals based on personal features such as age, gender, physical or mental constitution, and presumably race as well. However, it allows computer programs to reduce the number of personal injuries, and this is left quite broadly, so programmers are free to program this in whatever way they choose. This harks back to the trolley problem and it is unfortunate that Guideline 9 effectively sanctions consequentialism in programming. It is not possible for a work of this size to analyse all of the problems and issues arising from adopting a consequentialist approach. The works of philosophers such as Philippa Foot and Elizabeth Anscombe[21] have well highlighted the problems and dangers of adopting consequentialist approaches.

The only caveat in Guideline 9 is that non-involved parties must not be sacrificed. However, the larger question remains as to how 'non-involved parties' are defined, and whether and how this can be programmed. Take the example of the trolley problem. Arguably, the one man working on the track could be regarded as a non-involved party if the trolley was originally scheduled to head towards the track with five men working on it. Would the software be able to distinguish this and other kinds of non-involvement? Or perhaps this is a legal question that the programmer would not be aware of, and the programmer would proceed as if the one man on the other track is an involved party because all six men are working on the tracks?

---

[20]   Ibid.
[21]   See for example, Philippa Foot, *Moral Dilemmas and Other Topics in Moral Philosophy* (Clarendon Press 2002); Philippa Foot (n 2); G E M Anscombe, *Human Life, Action and Ethics: Essays by G. E. M. Anscombe*, edited by Mary Geach and Luke Gormally (Imprint Academic 2005); G E M Anscombe, *Intention* (Harvard University Press 2000); G E M Anscombe, *Metaphysics and the Philosophy of Mind: Collected Philosophical Papers Volume II* (Blackwell 1981).

Guideline 9 is extremely problematic and there will probably be litigation in the future to test its soundness.

6.10.   GUIDELINE 10[22]

In the case of automated and connected driving systems, the accountability that was previously the sole preserve of the individual shifts from the motorist to the manufacturers and operators of the technological systems and to the bodies responsible for taking infrastructure, policy and legal decisions. Statutory liability regimes and their fleshing out in the everyday decisions taken by the courts must sufficiently reflect this transition.

Guideline 10 is a welcome statement on the shift of liability to manufacturers and others who hold the keys to autonomous vehicles and the system that supports them. The shift is a logical one given that drivers have little to be accountable for in situations when their vehicles are autonomous.

6.11.   GUIDELINE 11[23]

Liability for damage caused by activated automated driving systems is governed by the same principles as in other product liability. From this, it follows that manufacturers or operators are obliged to continuously optimize their systems and also to observe systems they have already delivered and to improve them where this is technologically possible and reasonable.

Guideline 11 too is a welcome affirmation shining the spotlight on manufacturer's liability for the safety of their products, as well as putting the onus on manufacturers to continuously optimize, monitor and improve their products.

6.12.   GUIDELINE 12[24]

The public is entitled to be informed about new technologies and their deployment in a sufficiently differentiated manner. For the practical implementation of the principles developed here, guidance for the deployment and programming of automated vehicles should be derived in a form that is as transparent as possible, communicated in public and reviewed by a professionally suitable independent body.

Transparency, dissemination of information and review of developments and deployments seem to be the ethical call in Guideline 12. The education of the

---

[22]   Ethics Commission (n 9), 11.
[23]   Ibid, 12.
[24]   Ibid.

public on autonomous vehicle matters is a necessity to engender public trust in the systems. An independent body reviewing the practices and deployment will also ensure that companies developing autonomous vehicles do not mislead the general public, or deploy or program the autonomous vehicle in a manner contrary to the guidelines.

6.13. GUIDELINE 13[25]

It is not possible to state today whether, in the future, it will be possible and expedient to have the complete connectivity and central control of all motor vehicles within the context of a digital transport infrastructure, similar to that in the rail and air transport sectors. The complete connectivity and central control of all motor vehicles within the context of a digital transport infrastructure is ethically questionable if, and to the extent that, it is unable to safely rule out the total surveillance of road users and manipulation of vehicle control.

Guideline 13 appears to be wary of the ethical and other dangers of total surveillance that may arise if autonomous vehicles are completely connected and under central control where manipulation of vehicle control is possible. It does not, however, suggest that complete connectivity and central control should be prohibited.

6.14. GUIDELINE 14[26]

Automated driving is justifiable only to the extent to which conceivable attacks, in particular manipulation of the IT system or innate system weaknesses, do not result in such harm as to lastingly shatter people's confidence in road transport.

Guideline 14 serves as a warning and reminder that cybersecurity is a key issue and cyberattacks can be a reality. This guideline effectively warns that the computer systems security on autonomous vehicles should be watertight, as any harm caused by autonomous vehicles may lead to them being completely shunned by the public.

6.15. GUIDELINE 15[27]

Permitted business models that avail themselves of the data that are generated by automated and connected driving and that are significant or insignificant to vehicle control come up against their limitations in the autonomy and data sovereignty of

---

[25] Ibid.
[26] Ibid.
[27] Ibid.

road users. It is the vehicle keepers and vehicle users who decide whether their vehicle data that are generated are to be forwarded and used. The voluntary nature of such data disclosure presupposes the existence of serious alternatives and practicability. Action should be taken at an early stage to counter a normative force of the factual, such as that prevailing in the case of data access by the operators of search engines or social networks.

Guideline 15 appears to assert that vehicle data that is generated belongs to the users and keepers of a vehicle and they are the ones who should make the decision as to whether the data should be forwarded and used. This appears to be adapted from the privacy by design principle from the EU General Data Protection Regulation.[28] However, there may be practical problems with implementing this on autonomous vehicles. As already expounded in Chapters 2–4, autonomous vehicles with lidars rely on HD maps of its surroundings and these are constantly referenced by the vehicle against the updated maps to ensure the autonomous vehicle safely navigates its environment. If a user or keeper of an autonomous vehicle refuses for the data generated by its autonomous vehicle to be shared, then the vehicle may have difficulty navigating the roads.

6.16. GUIDELINE 16[29]

It must be possible to clearly distinguish whether a driverless system is being used or whether a driver retains accountability with the option of overruling the system. In the case of non-driverless systems, the human–machine interface must be designed such that at any time it is clearly regulated and apparent on which side the individual responsibilities lie, especially the responsibility for control. The distribution of responsibilities (and thus of accountability), for instance with regard to the time and access arrangements, should be documented and stored. This applies especially to the human-to-technology handover procedures. International standardization of the handover procedures and their documentation (logging) is to be sought in order to ensure the compatibility of the logging or documentation obligations as automotive and digital technologies increasingly cross national borders.

Guideline 16 contains a number of design stipulations. First, drivers must be allowed to drive and take over the driving function from the autonomous vehicle. Second, it must be very clear who is driving, the autonomous vehicle

---

[28] Regulation (EU) 2016/679 of the European Parliament and of the Council of 27 April 2016 on the protection of natural persons with regard to the processing of personal data and on the free movement of such data, and repealing Directive 95/46/EC (General Data Protection Regulation) <https://eur-lex.europa.eu/legal-content/EN/TXT/?uri=uriserv:OJ.L_.2016.119.01.0001.01.ENG&toc=OJ:L:2016:119:TOC> accessed 13 May 2018.

[29] Ethics Commission (n 9), 13.

or the human driver. This human–machine interface is perhaps to avoid any confusion the driver may have that the autonomous system is driving when it is not, thereby causing accidents. Third, the handover procedures from machine to human and vice versa should be clear as these will determine who is responsible and accountable should things go wrong. Fourth, data containing all such details should be appropriately stored.

Guideline 16 sets out clear and sensible rules in the practical aspects of the roles and responsibilities in the task of driving that will help minimize misunderstandings in the driving task and minimize accidents. The requirement that the data should be preserved will not only assist in liability questions, but will also help keep autonomous vehicle manufacturers accountable in the design of their autonomous vehicles.

6.17. GUIDELINE 17[30]

The software and technology in highly automated vehicles must be designed such that the need for an abrupt handover of control to the driver ('emergency') is virtually obviated. To enable efficient, reliable and secure human–machine communication and prevent overload, the systems must adapt more to human communicative behaviour rather than requiring humans to enhance their adaptive capabilities.

Guideline 17 espouses a level of technology that is almost perfect without the need for human drivers to suddenly take control of the vehicle. It appears to assume that there will be no emergencies in autonomous vehicle driving, which is an extremely high standard for the developers of autonomous vehicles to meet. Guideline 17 also suggests that if humans are required to take over the control of the autonomous vehicle, then it must not be an abrupt handover and that it needs to be a smooth handover with a certain time lag. Interestingly, Guideline 17 also stipulates that the machine must adapt more to human communicative behaviour and not the other way round. From this, it appears that Guideline 17 is also mandating that the design of the technology be more user-friendly.

6.18. GUIDELINE 18[31]

Learning systems that are self-learning in vehicle operation and their connection to central scenario databases may be ethically allowed if, and to the extent that, they generate safety gains. Self-learning systems must not be deployed unless they meet the safety requirements regarding functions relevant to vehicle control and do not

---

[30] Ibid.
[31] Ibid.

undermine the rules established here. It would appear advisable to hand over relevant scenarios to a central scenario catalogue at a neutral body in order to develop appropriate universal standards, including any acceptance tests.

Guideline 18 is rather intriguing. It only allows machine learning algorithms where they generate safety gains. Given that machine learning algorithms are an essential part of autonomous vehicle systems, this seems to suggest that all of the training datasets must be of quality and must ensure safety gains. Further, the actual algorithms themselves, including the mathematical and statistical models, must also ensure safety gains. This is indeed a very high standard for manufacturers to meet, similar to the standard of care espoused in Chapters 4 and 5, but it is unclear how the German regulators will be able to enforce this.

Guideline 18 also does not appear to take into consideration the dynamic nature of machine learning algorithms – it assumes that the deployment will be static with its reference to a one-off meeting of the safety requirements regarding functions relevant to vehicle control.

6.19. GUIDELINE 19[32]

In emergency situations, the vehicle must autonomously, i.e. without human assistance, enter into a 'safe condition'. Harmonization, especially of the definition of a safe condition or of the handover routines, is desirable.

Guideline 19 is a common sense requirement. If the autonomous vehicle can no longer function in the driving task, it must enter a safe condition, although there is no definition of what is a safe condition. This question must not be left to computer programmers alone to determine as programmers may not themselves be drivers and will not be experts at determining what would constitute a safe condition.

6.20. GUIDELINE 20[33]

The proper use of automated systems should form part of people's general digital education. The proper handling of automated driving systems should be taught in an appropriate manner during driving tuition and tested.

Guideline 20 stipulates the need for changes in driver education. This is definitely required given the spate of accidents in the US and China involving

---

[32] Ibid.
[33] Ibid.

Tesla vehicles and owners who may not have handled their vehicles properly. Drivers need to understand the limits of their vehicles and how to operate the autonomous vehicles safely, as well as the dangers the autonomous vehicle can cause.

6.21. MISSING PRINCIPLES: TRANSPARENCY AND TRUST IN PROGRAMMING

The 20 guidelines present a relatively sound set of ethical rules to follow with only a few of the guidelines being problematic.

Two glaring omissions from the guidelines are the principles of transparency and trust in the development of autonomous vehicle software. Both transparency and trust are critical and related: transparency will lead to an entry level of trust, both for regulators and the general public.

With transparency in the programming code, a regulator can more easily check what the programmers have programmed. Even with the machine learning algorithms, mandating transparency will help in determining why a computer program performs the way it does. Transparency can be programmed into software with something akin to an on–off switch, so that when regulators wish to check, they can flip the 'on' switch. It is also a very useful software debugging tool, especially to find bugs in the program that may lead to security breaches. Whilst transparency does not obviate the need for line-by-line programming code checking, it can speed up the process of software code checking substantially.

When there is transparency on how an autonomous vehicle functions, for example, that it will stop at a red traffic light, there will naturally come a greater level of trust in the autonomous system. However, it does not end there. Having trustworthy, well-working systems that function well is not sufficient. To truly enable trust, the design of autonomous systems also should have the capacity to explain decisions and to have recourse options when things go amiss.[34]

If people can understand how an autonomous system functions, even in situations where there might be some unpredictability, this will support trust in the autonomous system. The explanations, however, need to be comprehensible and accessible.[35]

---

[34] Michael Winikoff, 'How to make robots that we can trust', *The Conversation* (29 August 2017) <https://theconversation.com/how-to-make-robots-that-we-can-trust-79525> accessed 13 May 2018.

[35] Ibid.

Having recourse options means that victims of autonomous systems must be compensated in some way. One way this can be achieved that has already been canvassed in Chapter 5 is through the mechanism of strict liability.[36] Strict liability of course may, in modern liability structures, result in reliance on insurance schemes.

Autonomous vehicles will never be 100 per cent perfect,[37] contrary to what many people may have been misled into believing. Hence compensation is a necessary requirement as it enables the general public to trust an imperfect system.

Trust is a necessary ethical principle as it is the only way to ensure a sustainable and viable acceptance, deployment and take-up of autonomous vehicles.

6.22. ETHICS ENLARGED

The development of autonomous vehicles is still at a relatively early stage and there remain many other ethical issues that need to be addressed, including questions of under what circumstances we ought to allow autonomous vehicles to be tested on public roads. For example, should anyone who applies for a licence to test their autonomous vehicles, however undeveloped, be allowed to test them on public roads? The Tesla vehicles and the accidents to date raise the issue of software in beta-testing mode.[38] Should an autonomous vehicle with beta-testing-stage software be allowed on public roads to be faced by unsuspecting pedestrians and other road users? The intuitive answer should be no. Beta-testing of autonomous vehicles should not be undertaken by the general public as it is an activity that poses high risks of death and bodily injuries. Autonomous vehicles are not stationary objects like desktop computers, which will generally not kill people if the beta software malfunctions.

Other ethical issues might relate to the need for at least two safety drivers to be on-board the autonomous vehicle. Should autonomous vehicles be allowed to be tested on public roads without a safety driver inside the vehicle? Can the remote control of autonomous vehicles be trusted at this stage? What happens if the remote connection to the autonomous vehicle is lost, either due to a programming bug or due to a malicious attack by hackers? What if the WiFi connection to the autonomous vehicle has problems and loses connectivity with the test vehicle?

---

[36] See Chapter 5, Sections 5.5–5.7.
[37] Michael Winikoff (n 34).
[38] See Chapter 3.

Given the accident involving Uber's autonomous vehicle which had its emergency braking system disabled,[39] is it ethical or responsible for a developmental autonomous vehicle which has its emergency braking system disabled to be tested on public roads?

Indeed, it appears the governments in the US have been rushing through the autonomous vehicle race such that they seem to have sidestepped fundamental ethical issues and responsibilities. Given the high risks of computer security breaches and terrorist acts using autonomous vehicles,[40] it does not require complex ethical considerations to realize that autonomous vehicle testing should be done with a safety driver and functional brake pedal, accelerator and steering wheel. In fact, any other course of action would be irresponsible and unethical at this point in time. It is very surprising that the AV Start Bill has been moving swiftly through the hands of US lawmakers.[41] This bill, if passed, amongst other things, would allow manufacturers to omit steering wheels and brake pedals on their autonomous vehicles.[42]

These ethical questions and ethical responsibilities and many more need to be addressed, and they are just as acute as, if not more urgent than, ethical problems such as the trolley problem.

---

[39]   NTSB, *Preliminary Report Highway HWY18MH010* (n 13).
[40]   See Chapter 5.
[41]   Andrew J Hawkins, 'The fate of the steering wheel hangs in the balance', *The Verge* (16 March 2018) <https://www.theverge.com/2018/3/16/17130190/av-start-legislation-lobbying-washington-feinstein> accessed 13 May 2018.
[42]   Ibid.

7. For a smoother ride…

The development of autonomous vehicles does indeed hold promise of a very exciting future where the rate of accidents will be reduced when autonomy is matured to a certain level. However, how that stage can be reached is not entirely clear, especially given that massive amounts of on-road testing of autonomous vehicles are required.

What is clear at the present is that the promise of safety is currently not yet proven, either statistically[1] or scientifically.[2] An autonomous system based on an imprecise science such as statistics carries inherent risks and can and will make mistakes, just like human drivers do. Autonomous vehicles currently are not safer than human drivers. The technology has not reached readiness yet. The developers of autonomous vehicles need to honestly convince themselves and the general public that their systems actually work, that they are reliable under all kinds of conditions such as road construction works, glaring sun, wind and pouring rain, and that autonomous vehicles are indeed safe, and safer than human drivers.

The systems and features that are used in autonomous vehicles to supposedly make them safer have already been installed on some conventional vehicles for a number of years, such as emergency braking systems, adaptive cruise control, and active lane keeping.[3] Other components that are fitted on autonomous vehicles can also be incorporated into and adapted on conventional vehicles to increase their safety armoury.

The real promise of autonomous vehicles, if developed to a satisfactorily safe standard, is not about safety but it is about convenience. Many, however, do not realize that developing an autonomous vehicle that can drive every-

---

[1] David Shepardson, 'U.S. safety agency: Prior probe did not assess "effectiveness" of Tesla Autopilot', *Reuters* (3 May 2018) <https://www.reuters.com/article/tesla-autopilot/us-safety-agency-prior-probe-did-not-assess-effectiveness-of-tesla-autopilot-idUSL1N1S91XY> accessed 5 May 2018; Alex Roy, 'The half-life of danger: The truth behind the Tesla Model X crash', *The Drive* (16 April 2018) <http://www.thedrive.com/opinion/20082/the-half-life-of-danger-the-truth-behind-the-tesla-model-x-crash> accessed 5 May 2018.
[2] Any system based on developmental statistical and mathematical models cannot be scientifically safe. See Chapters 2–5. See also Alex Roy (n 1).
[3] Alex Roy (n 1).

where is extremely challenging, and it should not be the first goal to aim for.[4] The biggest hurdle for autonomous driving is dealing with the edge cases, the curveballs that may happen every 10,000 miles or more of driving.[5] The reason for this is that machine learning may improve performance from 90 per cent accuracy to maybe 99.9 per cent, but it has not been able to improve further than that to say, 99.9999 per cent accuracy.[6] It is for this reason that building an autonomous vehicle that can safely navigate the continuously changing driving environment with many changing variables will be difficult.

7.1.   DRIVERLESS TRUCKS IN AUSTRALIA

Autonomous vehicles can and have been used in limited or remote settings to fill a need, improve efficiency and profitability, and even improve the safety of a work environment. In Western Australia, several mining companies have been using driverless trucks for a number of years in remote rural areas to transport mining materials.[7] These driverless trucks are not used on public roads, but only at the mining sites.

At mining sites, it can be dangerous for workers to be walking around when gigantic trucks are driving about hauling materials. The often uneven terrain can also make it dangerous for a human truck driver to operate the truck, as the truck may tip over when the terrain is hostile. This is where autonomous trucks can bring safety and efficiency, not to mention increased productivity and profitability.[8] Autonomous trucks are able to drive a more or less exact route every time without getting bored or tired, or needing to take time off due to fatigue. The driverless trucks can work 24 hours a day, 7 days a week without rest and with minimal errors, hauling millions of tonnes of mining materials

---

    [4]   Andrew Ng, 'Andrew Ng: When will self-driving cars be on roads?', *Quora* (30 January 2016) <https://www.quora.com/Andrew-Ng-When-will-self-driving-cars-be -on-roads?no_redirect=1> accessed 5 May 2018.
    [5]   Ibid.
    [6]   Ibid.
    [7]   Stuart McKinnon, 'Rio Tinto's driverless trucks program shifts gear to make Pilbara mine full auto', *The West Australian* (18 December 2017) <https://thewest .com.au/business/mining/rio-tintos-driverless-trucks-program-shifts-gear-to-make -pilbara-mine-full-auto-ng-b88693612z>; Stuart McKinnon, 'Nobody at the wheel at BHP's Jimblebar iron ore mine site', *The West Australian* (7 July 2017) <https:/ /thewest.com.au/news/wa/nobody-at-the-wheel-at-bhps-jimblebar-iron-ore-mine-site -ng-b88529442z> accessed 5 May 2018.
    [8]   Peter Klinger, 'Robot trucks outperform human drivers: Rio', *The West Australian* (15 October 2015) <https://thewest.com.au/business/finance/robot-trucks -outperform-human-drivers-rio-ng-ya-159244> accessed 5 May 2018.

every year. Fewer workers are required at the mining site and workers are located out of harm's way.[9]

A central computer system at the mining site directs each truck to a particular shovel to load, and thereafter to a particular dumping point. Each dump location is recorded so that no two loads are dumped into the same pile. The central computer system is also programmed with scheduling and assignment algorithms designed to maximize productivity and meet each day's loading goals.[10]

The driverless trucks have also been fitted with sufficient sensors to detect a human, or even a kangaroo, in their path and are programmed to slow down or stop to avoid a collision – kangaroos are native to outback Australia and are often encountered at mining sites in Western Australia.[11]

What this example shows is that it is possible to deploy autonomous systems safely. In the driverless truck example, the trucks are deployed at mining sites – a controlled environment. The controlled environment also means that it is possible to keep variables to a minimum. Importantly, the risk of injury or harm to humans can be minimized to practically zero as there are very few humans who are in the physical proximity of the driverless trucks.

7.2. CONTROLLED ENVIRONMENTS

Apart from mining sites, how else can autonomous vehicles be deployed safely and in a controlled environment? For a start, the road infrastructure would need improvement so that it is more easily and clearly understood by autonomous vehicles. Road surfaces and lane markings need to be well maintained, and there must be no construction works with detours or portable traffic lights, which would confuse autonomous vehicles. Autonomous vehicles are not built to detect large potholes and uncovered manholes,[12] so they will simply drive over or into them.

A good controlled environment might be a campus or some other small area that is well demarcated, namely precinct based. To make economic sense and be environmentally sustainable, it would ideally be a bus or shuttle able to transport more than one person around a loop or a single route. This at least

---

[9]   John Morell, 'Self-driving mining trucks', *Mechanical Engineering Magazine* (March 2017) <https://www.asme.org/engineering-topics/articles/robotics/selfdriving -mining-trucks> accessed 5 May 2018.

[10]   Ibid.

[11]   Ibid.

[12]   Lee Gomes, 'Hidden obstacles for Google's self-driving cars', *MIT Technology Review* (28 August 2014) <https://www.technologyreview.com/s/530276/hidden -obstacles-for-googles-self-driving-cars/> accessed 5 May 2018.

minimizes how much road infrastructure would need to be improved. Being a single route, it could also be easily well publicized to road users in the small area, so that they would be more aware of the autonomous vehicle in their road use in that area. If the autonomous shuttle can handle the road environment safely and effectively in that single route, including avoiding hitting pedestrians and cyclists but ignoring flying paper bags, then additional routes could be added slowly and gradually.

An example of where this is being implemented is in Sydney, Australia, where a shuttle will run autonomously on a pre-programmed route in a small precinct.[13] A highly automated Level 4 passenger shuttle at Sydney Olympic Park began trials in 2017 and the trial is ongoing with three stages. The first stage of the trial involved tests and safety checks of the shuttle bus in an enclosed off-road environment at Newington Armoury near the former Olympic village, that is, private roads away from pedestrians. The trial is currently at stage two where the public can use the shuttle as it makes the rounds on a closed section of the Sydney Olympic Park precinct. By July 2018, it will reach stage three, where the shuttle is expected to operate live on the roads at Sydney Olympic Park, where office workers and other members of the public will ride the driverless shuttle.[14]

The trial will collect information on infrastructure, supporting technology and how customers interact with the autonomous vehicle. This will be used to further improve the system and guide possible wider deployment.[15]

The Smart Shuttle, as it is called, is built by French company Navya, has the capacity to carry up to 15 passengers and runs on electricity. It uses on-board lidar and radar systems with high-definition three-dimensional maps of the route environment. It has a maximum speed of 45 kilometres per hour, but for the trial, the shuttle will operate at around 20 kilometres per hour, a deliberate decision to ensure safety.[16]

7.3.   FINAL THOUGHTS

This work has attempted to make the technology and the science behind autonomous vehicles accessible. Much of the legal literature to date and perhaps

---

[13]   NSW Government, 'Driverless vehicle projects' <https://www.transport.nsw.gov .au/projects/programs/smart-innovation-centre/driverless-vehicle-projects> accessed 5 May 2018.

[14]   NSW Government, 'Smart Shuttle Trial Fact Sheet' <https://www.transport.nsw .gov.au/system/files/media/documents/2017/sic-automated-shuttle-launch-fact-sheet -aug-2017.pdf> accessed 5 May 2018.

[15]   Ibid.

[16]   Ibid.

even regulatory decisions have been based on misconceptions fuelled by a lack of knowledge of the underlying science and basis of the technology. One must at least have a basic understanding of the beast that one is trying to regulate.

The use of tort liability as a framework for discussion in this work was chosen because negligence is a doctrine that is not unfamiliar in numerous jurisdictions. Further, the concept of the reasonable person is one that is intrinsically valuable, and that each one of us, being human and not machine, would understand. It carries the expectation of treating others, and being treated oneself, with the dignity, respect and safety due to a human being.

Tort liability, especially as it relates to cybersecurity, is also pertinent for industry as it serves as a useful means of incentivizing close adherence to industry best practices. Cybersecurity is only as strong as its weakest link, and hence, cybersecurity must be a fundamental part of the entire design process, not merely an afterthought.

As one motor vehicle expert has put it, '[a]t current levels of technology, companies are selling convenience at the expense of safety', referring to the systems on vehicles such as the Autopilot on the Tesla and SuperCruise on the Cadillac. As industry advances towards fully autonomous driving, premature systems should not be allowed to be unleashed onto the general public on public roads until they are fully developed, not during the process of perfecting them.

Self-regulation and self-certification by private companies is never a good idea when the safety of the general public is at stake, thus it is the role of responsible governments to fulfil their duties and to govern. A regulator must discharge its duties in protecting citizens; this is the minimum ethical conduct required, amongst many other ethical responsibilities in connection with autonomous vehicles.

Index